Doing
GOOD *for*
GOODNESS'
SAKE

Doing
GOOD *for*
GOODNESS'
SAKE

*Heartwarming Stories
and Inspiring Ideas
to Help You Help Others*

STEVE ZIKMAN

Inner Ocean Publishing, Inc.
Maui, Hawai'i · San Francisco, California

Inner Ocean Publishing, Inc.
P.O. Box 1239
Makawao, Maui, HI 96768-1239

Publisher Cataloging-in-Publication Data
Zikman, Steve.
Doing good for goodness' sake : heartwarming stories and inspiring
ideas to help you help others / Steve Zikman.—Makawao, Hawaii :
Inner Ocean, 2004.
p.   cm.
Includes index.

ISBN: 1-9730722-39-7

1. Helping behavior. 2. Helping behavior—Anecdotes.
3. Caring. 4. Altruism. 5. Interpersonal relations.
6. Empathy. 7. Conduct of life.
8. Assistance in emergencies. I. Title.
BF637.H4 Z54 2004
158/.3—dc22 0409

For information on bulk purchases, promotions, fund-raising,
premiums, or educational use, please contact: Special Markets,
866.731.2216 or sales@innerocean.com

Dedicated to my parents,
Thelma and Joel Zikman,
for being beacons of unconditional love

Contents

Chapter 1

EVERYDAY GOOD

Chapter 2

FIRST RESPONSE

Chapter 3

THROUGH THE EYES OF A CHILD

Chapter 4

TEEN TALK

Chapter 5

FOR THE HOLIDAYS

Chapter 6

MISSIONS OF THE HEART

How wonderful it is that nobody need wait a single moment before starting to improve their world.

ANNE FRANK

Foreword

When UNICEF asked me in 1987 to represent them as an International Goodwill Ambassador, I saw it as a way to respond to a moral imperative. In the role of Ambassador, I would be given the opportunity to make a difference in the lives of children and offer my voice and unwavering commitment to them. At the time of my appointment I had no idea where the journey would take me, but I well understood the importance of my decision. Beyond worldwide concert halls and movie theaters, my experiences could help make the world a safer place for children.

I remember my first mission for UNICEF, to Dakar, Senegal. As chairman of the International Symposium of Artists and Intellectuals for African Children, I helped organize the largest fundraising concert ever held in Sub-Saharan Africa. Alongside more than 20 other artists, we garnered the collective power of culture and celebrity to spread a message of hope to millions of African children suffering from hunger and poverty. In 1985, I was part of a similar group of artists. You may remember the "We Are the World" global mobilization? Two years later, in the capital city of Dakar, I looked back on what I'd learned from that life-changing experience to guide us toward another successful event.

The next 17 years proved to be a dynamic and industrious time for me as I travelled the world, supporting UNICEF's efforts by participating in fundraising and advocacy events, and by speaking on behalf of children whenever the opportunity presented itself. My passion for children's rights has carried me far and wide, crisscrossing the globe and meeting children the world over. Their wish to see change in the world, and their unflinching faith in its promise, has been an inspiration to me.

In 1994, as civil strife erupted on a massive scale in Rwanda, ending in the deaths of an estimated 500,000-800,000 people, I travelled there on a mission for UNICEF. During my stay in Rwanda, I met the newly named president Pasteur Bizimungo, and visited UNICEF-supported centers for unaccompanied children. Upon my return to the United States, UNICEF used me to launch a full-scale media campaign to bring awareness to the needs of Rwandan children.

In the summer of 2001, as the latest terror of our century continued to kill our young leaving thousands orphaned, I travelled to South Africa. There, I witnessed first-hand the impact of HIV/AIDS, and the efforts being made to combat this deadly scourge. When I returned to New York City, I publicized the mission and promoted UNICEF's efforts via the media and other venues.

On a recent trip to Kenya, I witnessed once again the difference one person can make in the lives of others. As I visited a local school one afternoon, to my delight, two children approached me. Bending my knees to meet their eyes, weary with confusion and sadness, I listened closely as they explained to me that their school was in the process of being sold. Assuming they would continue their education at another school, I asked them where its new location would be. Their reply stunned me. These little girls explained that once the school closed there would be no replacement facility. I understood it was my duty to ensure them a better future, one where education would become a fundamental right.

The next day, I was scheduled to meet with the head of state, President Kibaki. I shared with him what I had learned from the children. By the end of the meeting I had the assurance of the President and government officials that funding would be available to ensure the children's education would continue without interruption.

I am happy to report that in 2003, Kenya made the bold decision to abolish school fees, further advancing the rights of all children to receive an education. As a result, families who had once been unable to afford the old levies of $133, began sending their children to school. Almost overnight, more than 1.3 million children entered school.

The year 2004 marks fifty years since UNICEF appointed its first Goodwill Ambassador, comedian and entertainer Danny Kaye. I am proud to follow in his footsteps, and grateful to the children I've met along the way-each of whom has deepened and enriched my own life.

Almost two decades after my official appointment as a Goodwill Ambassador, what I know for certain is that each of us has the power to make a difference in the world. The challenge is to envision the kind of world we'd like to live in, and commit our hearts and souls to bringing about that change. Once we do that, there's no telling what we can do and where we can go.

Harry Belafonte, UNICEF Goodwill Ambassador

Introduction

Chance favors the prepared mind.
LOUIS PASTEUR

I READ A BEAUTIFUL AND TOUCHING story about how the community of Gander, Newfoundland, cared for thousands of reluctant visitors whose planes had been diverted there on the morning of September 11, 2001. By the time the last of the thirty-eight jets had landed at the small airport, more than 6,500 passengers were in need of food and shelter in this town of 9,600 residents.

Everyone came out in full force to help wherever they could. People of all nationalities were treated like close friends as the locals opened their homes, hearts, and wallets. They rallied as one to give the visitors beds, showers, food, drinks, clothing, and access to telephones and computers so the visitors could tell loved ones they were safe.

One traveler was on her way home to Chicago and stayed with a family in Gambo, a village near Gander. "They invited us up in the woods for a barbeque," she recalled, "*and* we made burgers and hot dogs *and* had a few beers *and* kissed the cod *and* became honorary Newfoundlanders!"

On that clear autumn day, ordinary people were called upon to do the extraordinary—the instinctive response of an open heart. They didn't expect anything in return; they simply did what needed to be done.

Author and lecturer Leo Buscaglia once talked about a contest he was asked to judge. The purpose of the contest was to find the most caring child. The winner was a four-year-old child whose next-door neighbor was an elderly gentleman who had recently lost his wife. Upon seeing the man cry, the little boy went into the old gentleman's yard, climbed onto his lap, and just sat there. When his mother asked him what he had said to the neighbor, the little boy said, "Nothing. I just helped him cry."

From the extraordinary events of Gander, Newfoundland, to the little boy and his neighbor, we all are presented with a myriad of opportunities to do good. All too often, however, we fail to see the need that is right before our eyes, or if we see it, we fail to act. We may feel overwhelmed, or think that someone else will take care of it or that whatever we have to offer isn't enough.

It is my hope that the stories and material in this book will demonstrate that there are many ways to make a difference. I have divided the selections into six easily accessible chapters: Everyday Good, First Response, For the Holidays, Through the Eyes of a Child, Teen Talk, and Missions of the Heart. These pieces address not only situations that fall into our laps but also ways in which people can assume a more active role by volunteering their time and energy and changing the world for the better.

Each story is followed by a call to action. I thought it was important to include not only inspiring stories but also useful suggestions to help you turn that inspiration into action, to anticipate what might be needed in a given situation and to learn how you can prepare yourself, as well as your friends and family, to do what needs to be done.

In 1988, I was fortunate enough to meet Mother Teresa not once but twice over a period of two days—the second time, by pure coincidence at 3:00 A.M. in a dark airport lounge in Bombay. We talked for about an hour—just she and I—and in that brief encounter, she told me about her missions across the world. She knew each mission intimately, and especially what each one needed—beds, blankets, a refrigerator, a plot of land for a new orphanage. She knew every detail without the benefit of notes or an Excel spreadsheet. It was all in her head, and in her heart. Even though she was close to eighty years of age and in poor health, she knew what was needed and did it. She was always prepared. Little was left to chance; much was left to faith.

I have told this story many times, and, recently, someone asked if, in meeting her, I thought that Mother Teresa was a spiritual person. Now, of course I knew that she must have been a spiritual person, but I must say that I didn't feel a spiritual sense emanating from her. Rather there was a spirituality existing all *around* her. In speaking with her, I felt as if I were talking to a businesswoman. She was all action.

Before I left Mother Teresa to return to her prayers, she offered these words: "There is so much to do and so little time." We hear this sentiment often, but coming from her, it took on extra meaning. In the time that has passed since meeting Mother Teresa, I have searched for ways to apply her spirit in my own life, but let's face it: It's pretty hard to do as she did. We're not all saints. At least, I'm not.

Over the years, I have tried to make a difference. As an eleven-year-old growing up in Montreal, I got my sixth grade class to start a branch of the Society to Overcome Pollution (S.T.O.P.). I have participated in grassroots politics, volunteered as a Big Brother, served dinner to the homeless, and run a few charity races. But like you, I'm busy and find myself trying to juggle many things, hoping to fit in some time to help others—when I can. Mother Teresa knew of what she spoke: Time *is* short.

So, we don't have to save the world. Just do our part—with our hands, with our feet, with our minds, with our mouths, with our ears, and, most important, with our hearts.

Steve Zikman

Chapter 1

EVERYDAY GOOD

*I cannot do all the good that the world needs,
but the world needs all the good that I can do.*

JANA STANFIELD

Gary's Mug

We must not only give what we have;
we must also give what we are.

DESIRE-JOSEPH MERCIER

I never saw the minivan that hit my Ford Tempo. The accident was clearly my fault. With my girlfriend trying to end our relationship, my father recently diagnosed with cancer, my mother on her deathbed two days before Christmas, and several of my siblings furious with me about her will, I never should have been driving in the first place. Fortunately, the other driver was a neighbor whose scratched bumper was more palatable than my crumpled fender. He saw the accident as too minor to report. I saw it as one more loose thread in the unraveling of my life.

Hauling my car into a nearby collision shop, I had never felt more despondent. The shop supervisor said that repairs would take four or five days. I wouldn't get my car back until a few days after Christmas. Heading home on the subway that afternoon, I doubted things could get any worse.

But they did.

My mother died on Christmas Eve; one of my brothers wished aloud that it were me in the casket instead of her; my father began his presurgical evaluations; and my pleas to my lover fell on deaf ears. When I returned to the collision shop a day or two after the funeral, I was an emotional wreck.

I needed somebody to listen, but I had no one. Unable

to stop myself, I unloaded everything on the shop supervisor. When I finished, there were tears in my eyes, but somehow I had kept myself from breaking down completely. It was then that I noticed his coffee cup.

> In its total land area of 21 square miles, Bermuda has six times more vehicle accidents per square mile than anywhere else in the world.

It was one of those multicolored mugs that translate a given name into several different languages. For the first time I realized the supervisor and I shared a first name. There it was—Gary—in French, Spanish, Hebrew, Italian, German, and Japanese.

Embarrassed at having shared so much with a stranger, I tried to start a new conversation and asked where he had gotten his mug.

"My mother gave it to me, and I want you to have it," he said. "She died this time last year. I know what you're going through."

When I refused his kind offer, he insisted, and I drove away from his shop with the mug that would hold my hot chocolate, tea, and sometimes wine as I spent the remainder of my semester break coming to terms with my losses.

My dad survived his surgery and is doing well. My siblings and I have since mended our relationships. I went on to another romance and eventually remarried. But I will never forget Gary at the collision shop. He gave me one of the nicest gifts I have ever received, not only the milk of human kindness but the cup in which to hold it.

Gary Earl Ross

 ## Find Creative Ways to Give Something to Someone Else

- Buy two movie tickets and some popcorn for a friend.

- Put some money into an expired parking meter.

- Send someone a small gift with a handcrafted card.

- Buy a subscription to your favorite magazine for a family member or friend.

- At a tollbooth, pay for the car behind you.

- Toss a few extra items into your shopping cart at the grocery store for someone who can't afford them.

- Take pictures of someone you know, choose the best ones, and give the person copies, all handsomely framed.

- Give away unused furniture or appliances.

- Bake a cake and bring it to an overworked friend or neighbor.

- Pay for a stranger's meal at a restaurant.

- On the next rainy day, take an extra umbrella and give it to somebody who doesn't have one.

Crossword Puzzle Man

There's someone out there who needs you.
You must live your life so that person can find you.

JAN PHILLIPS

I've seen him a few times, always on the same subway line. He wanders from passenger to passenger with his crossword puzzle, saying nothing, holding the newspaper out in front of him with a questioning look on his childlike face.

He's a tall man—well over 6 feet—with smooth skin the color of dark chocolate and eyes and hair as black as pitch. He laughs often, a low cackle, and for no apparent reason. Maybe he's laughing at jokes in his head. Maybe he's laughing at the subway riders annoyed at not finding any available seats. Maybe he's amused at the rocking of the subway, the sudden jolts that leave us scrambling for a bar to hold onto. More likely, though, his laughs have something to do with the crossword puzzle he clutches in both hands.

The first person he approaches refuses to look up at him. She's thinking, *Great, why do the morons always pick on me?* Still, he doesn't get discouraged. He stands there, his crossword puzzle extended, waiting for her to help him solve the next clue. Eventually he gives up and tries someone else, who gets up from his seat and makes his way through the crowd to the other end of the subway car. Crossword Puzzle Man follows him with his eyes, his lips parted in confusion.

It's the same every time I have seen him. People shy away from him, they ignore him, they refuse to meet his gaze. Perhaps they are afraid of his strangeness, perhaps disgusted by his retardation. He wanders up and down the subway cars, waiting in vain for someone to offer assistance. Who knows how long he has waited? Who knows how long he will wait? Yesterday, I would have said forever, but this morning on the Yonge Street subway line, something happened.

It was early, not yet eight o'clock, when I saw him making his way past the backpacks and bulky winter coats, his crossword puzzle in hand. I examined the other passengers, wondering which ones he would stop at. There were a couple of high school girls, a few university students who looked like they were on their way to class, a businessman staring anxiously at his cell phone, and an elderly woman, her hands filled with plastic bags. Which one would Crossword Puzzle Man choose?

I was disappointed when he stopped in front of a wealthy-looking middle-aged woman wearing a fur muff, her makeup applied immaculately. *She won't like this at all,* I thought. She's too proper, too done-up. She's not used to dealing with the wackos found on the public transit system.

But there he stopped, his shoulders stooped, his newspaper outstretched towards her, his eyebrows raised in question. I waited for the brush-off that would, inevitably, come.

"Oh hello!" she said cheerily, to my amazement.

He laughed his deep guffaw.

"How are you?" she asked, a smile forming on her lips.

Again, the laugh. I waited for her to look at me, to ask me with her eyes what the heck was going on with this weirdo.

"I see you are doing the crossword puzzle," she said, smiling all the time.

He laughed in response and thrust the newspaper closer to her face.

She nodded and examined the paper for a few seconds. One across. Cosmetics brand, Mary blank. "Do you know a makeup brand that starts with Mary?" she asked.

He cackled low.

She smiled at him. "No? Do you know Mary Kay?"

He looked at her with lips parted.

"Kay. K-A-Y. You write that in. K-A-Y. Right there." She indicated the spot on his puzzle.

He laughed again and pushed the newspaper and pencil at her.

"You want me to do it?"

Another low cackle.

She wrote it in for him and handed back the paper and pencil. Again, he waited in front of her, lips parted, questions all over his face.

"Let's see what two across is," she said.

They continued for several stops until it was time for her to get off. I looked around at the faces of the other riders as she filled in words and as he laughed at the joy of it all. The faces were almost all filled with smiles. It was partly amusement, but not completely. There was more to it. On a few of the faces, I read compassion for this young man, but there was something else. I just couldn't put my finger on it.

And then, just as the well-dressed lady was preparing to disembark from the subway car, it occurred to me.

Admiration.

On every face, there was admiration for that lady in the expensive fur muff.

She taught us all a lesson that morning. She taught us that being a Good Samaritan means not picking and choosing whom you help. It means offering assistance to anyone, even those who look different or act in ways that we don't understand. It means confronting our fears about those who live on the fringes of our society, in places we never visit or think about. She taught us that being a Good Samaritan means helping anyone in need.

Even Crossword Puzzle Man.

Hayley Linfield

The world's largest crossword was published in 1982 by Robert Turcot of Quebec, Canada. It offered 12,489 clues across and 13,125 down. A few determined fans are still trying to fill in its 82,951 squares.

Reach Out to Others

- Buy some flowers for a stranger.

- Hold the door of the subway or bus for someone rushing to catch it.

- Write a note of appreciation to your mail carrier, waitress, or store clerk.

- Share something funny (an article, story, cartoon) with someone else.

- If you see someone who looks like she's lost something, help her out.

- Once a week, donate an hour of your time as a gift to someone else.

- When visiting a friend or family member in the hospital, spend a few minutes with someone else who has no visitors.

- Pass on a book or magazine article that you really liked to someone else.

- Write some kind words to someone who recently received sad news.

- While waiting in line at the grocery store, let someone go in front of you.

- Help dig someone's car out of the snow.

- If you ride the bus, buy a pastry and juice for your driver.

- Visit your local VA hospital—many veterans receive few, if any, visitors.
- Offer your taxi to others.

Deliverance

If a man be gracious and courteous to strangers,
it shows that he is a citizen of the world,
and that his heart is no island cut off from other lands,
but a continent that joins to them.

FRANCIS BACON

L iving the life of a pizza delivery man, I'd often find reason to rejoice. More than the occasional $5 or $10 tip were the smiles of the children waiting at the door, and every once in a while, the unexpected.

I had just pulled into the busy parking lot after a string of deliveries. As I neared the pizza parlor, I saw two people running toward me. A man and a woman, Asian looking, carrying big shopping bags emblazoned with the logo from one of the clothing stores that helped to anchor the strip mall. I turned into my parking stall, a few rows from the pizza parlor. I put the car in park and looked up. There they were, smiling, looking relieved.

All of a sudden, the back door of my car opened. I turned around. The couple had jumped into the backseat of my car. At first, I was confused as to why they would jump into a pizza delivery car; after all, it was evident from the sign on the top of the car that read "PIZZA" in large bold letters. Then it made sense. They couldn't read English; they saw the car-topper and thought I was a taxi. That had to be it.

I got out of the car. They looked bewildered and followed. I pointed to the pizza parlor. They realized their mistake. Obviously embarrassed, they laughed nervously and walked away. I went back into the store, thinking little of it.

A few minutes later, I stepped outside and noticed the same couple, across from me, looking like they were waiting for something. The woman walked away and a few seconds later she returned. I heard the phone ringing and took the call. A pickup. "Pie on screen," I told my coworker.

I went to the front window and looked out. Again, the woman walked away, the man shaking his head. A minute passed, the woman returned, now shaking her head. That's it—I must find out what's going on.

"I'll be right back," I called out.

Before I approached, the woman had walked away again. The man looked exasperated. I looked toward the Starbucks. The public phones. That's where the woman was. She returned.

"No taxi come," she said tearfully in what was obviously the few words that she knew in English.

I noticed a card in her hand. "Can I see?" I asked.

She handed it to me. It was from North Las Vegas Cab, miles and miles from where we were.

I had my cell phone and called the number. Busy signal. Tried again. Busy signal. I looked up at the couple; they looked exhausted, defeated.

"What country are you from?" I asked.

"Japan," the woman answered.

"Where are you staying?"

She looked at me, confused. "No understand."

"Hotel?"

She nodded sheepishly. She opened her purse, pulled out another card.

"Ah, the Mandalay Bay. Nice hotel," I replied. "How long have you been in Las Vegas?"

"Three day," the woman said, smiling. "First time, America."

I wish that I could take them to their hotel, I thought. But it was too far and I'm sure my boss wouldn't go for it. I was the only delivery guy. What I needed to do was to call another taxi service, one closer. There was a phone book in the pizza store. I motioned for the couple to follow me.

"Rest your legs," I said pointing to the chairs in the waiting area. They smiled and sat, relieved. They were exhausted and maybe hungry too.

I went around the counter and pulled out the phone book. I found the right number and dialed. "Where to?" said the dispatcher.

"Mandalay Bay."

"About twenty minutes," was the reply.

I related this to the woman who, in turn, relayed it in her Japanese to her husband. He nodded a sigh of relief.

I went around the counter back to the pick-up area. "Are you hungry?" I asked them, pointing up toward the big pizza sign.

"Yes, yes, yes," the woman answered.

"Would you like a pizza?"

The woman looked at the man, said something in Japanese. He smiled a very big smile.

"Yes, yes . . . cheese, cheese," the woman answered.

Some popular pizza toppings around the world are ginger in India, squid in Japan, green peas in Brazil, pineapple in Australia, and coconut in Costa Rica.

I put together a large cheese pizza, and slipped it into the oven.

"Six minutes," I said to the couple.

And then I asked them if they were thirsty.

"Yes, cola," the woman replied.

I pulled two 20-ounce bottles from the cooler, a few napkins, and two paper plates and handed them to my new friends. The woman rose, bowed slightly, and opened her purse. She pulled out a wad of American dollars of various denominations.

"No, no," I said. "On me."

She insisted. Again, I refused. "Please, pizza's on me. No charge."

She smiled, sat down.

When the pizza was ready, I sliced and boxed it before handing it to the Japanese couple.

The man drew a camera from his pocket. He took a picture of the pizza box and then had his wife pose with the two plates. Then he gestured for me to stand with his wife, and he took another picture.

The man opened the box, and with the hot steam rising, he took a deep breath and exhaled with a smile.

"Good, good, good," the woman said. And then she set her plate down and opened her purse. She pulled out a little notebook, rose, and handed it to me.

"You write address."

I wrote it down, and then a few minutes later, the cab arrived and the driver came in.

"Somebody call a cab?"

"Yes, please take my friends visiting from Japan to the Mandalay. They're tired. You know, they came over here to do some serious shopping."

He smiled.

Two weeks later, I received a package. Inside was a beautiful Japanese card inscribed with: "We had heard about American hospitality, but it was not until we met you that we had experienced it." Beneath the card was a beautiful tin containing an assortment of Japanese crackers. Three weeks before Christmas, it was my first and best present.

Rick Fico

The World Tourism Organization estimates that there were more than 702.6 million international travelers in 2002.

Help a Traveler or Tourist

- At or near popular tourist destinations, if you see someone reading a map, offer your assistance.

- Look out for confused travelers on the subway, train, or bus. Ask if they need help.

- Offer to carry heavy luggage, especially while getting on and off transportation.

- Help people who might need exact change for trains and buses.

- If a traveler is stranded and needs to place a phone call, offer to do it for him on your cell phone.

- If you know their language, assist in interpretation.

- Volunteer to take a photo for a group so that everyone may be included.

- Make recommendations to help tourists find favorite local restaurants, beaches, hikes, grocery stores, pharmacies, or accommodations.

- Be a tourist's guide for the day, and show her around your town.

- When someone you know is traveling, leave a kind note in his luggage.

- Buy a small souvenir for a tourist to take home.

Leave No Trace

Do your little bit of good where you are;
it's those little bits of good put together that
overwhelm the world.

ARCHBISHOP DESMOND TUTU

I was invited to join a group of longtime friends on one of their semiannual camping forays. The guy who invited me left me with the impression that the trips were somewhat civilized; however, I'd heard tales of drunken men traipsing around the woods, games played with fire, and even the occasional sport-shooting event. It sounded out of control, but I needed the getaway.

On Sunday morning, after a hearty breakfast, we left for Sugar Creek Canoes. They would drop us with our canoes a few miles upstream, so we could spend the day paddling back down to the pickup point.

The river was wide, and there was plenty of room for our four canoes to spread out. Soon, a friendly competition began, to see who could be in front of the pack. And, of course, there was the occasional ramming of an "enemy" canoe.

But Steve was a more serious canoeist. He was a quiet, reflective guy who rarely got into the adolescent antics of his fellow paddling buddies, often falling well behind the rest of the group. I watched as he wove his way along the river, at times steering his canoe into the bank. I wasn't sure what he was up to, but then I saw it. He'd spotted a discarded plastic milk jug in the weeds along the bank, picked it up, deposited it in his canoe, and proceeded to catch up with the rest of us.

From our conversations around the campfire, I learned that Steve was an avid hunter and fisherman. But he was also a camper and hiker, and appreciated the beauty of the outdoors.

During the rest of our trip down the river, I cannot count how many times I saw Steve and his canoeing partner stop along the bank, on a sandbar, or in the shallows to retrieve some object that shouldn't be there.

As Steve repeatedly fell behind and caught up again, he was the butt of good-natured joking for his obsessive behavior. But inside, we all admired him. Still, we had to laugh at the sheer volume—and weight—of the trash that he'd collected that day. And at some of the items we could see in his canoe. It was immersed nearly to the gunwales.

Eventually, we reached the pickup point, where we had to haul our canoes out of the water and up a steep hill to a shady area at the end of a country road. It took all of us to haul Steve's canoe up the hill, even after we had removed some of the garbage. In addition to multiple milk jugs, old tires, and rusty soft drink cans, there was a T-shirt, a hubcap, a toilet, and a half-inch-thick, 2-foot-square plate of steel.

The average American throws away 3.5 pounds of trash a day.

We still joke about that day thirteen years ago, but it also told us a lot about the dedicated protector of the environment that Steve was and continues to be. He's not one for Greenpeace, or lobbying, or attending protests on environmental issues. Rather, Steve is a warrior on the ground, making a difference everyday, wherever he finds himself in nature. Every year he participates in the Ohio River cleanup. He always takes a plastic grocery sack or Ziploc bag on any hike, because he knows he's going to be carrying back trash. And he's inspired the rest of us to do it, too. Because of him we all try to leave every natural place better than we found it.

Paraphrasing the outdoorsman motto of "Leave No Trace," one might say that Steve's motto is "Leave No Trash." But even that would be an understatement. His true mantra is "Leave No One's Trash."

D.D. Cummings

 ### Do an Everyday Act to Better the Environment

- Plant a tree.
- Help conserve water. Fix leaky taps and install water-saving devices in your home. Find alternative landscaping that requires less water.
- Learn more about composting and try it.
- Turn off all lights, computers, heaters, and fans when not in use.

- Focus on recycling within your household and workplace. Use the curbside pickup program if your community has one, or take your items to the local drop-off or buy-back center.

- Cut back on the number of food products that result in nonrecyclables. Have a "litterless" lunch.

- Use your car more efficiently. Do as many things as possible in one trip. Don't leave your car running, and keep it properly tuned. Carpool or, even better, leave your car at home and walk, ride your bike, or take the bus.

- Shop for products in containers that can be recycled and for items that can be repaired or reused.

- Support recycling markets by buying and using products made from recycled materials.

- Learn more about recycling:

  National Recycling Coalition: www.nrc-recycle.org
  Time to Recycle: www.timetorecycle.org

Celebrity Makeovers

*Treat people as if they were what they should be,
and you help them become what they are
capable of becoming.*

GOETHE

A friend decided to end her skin-care and makeup home party sales business and return all the unused products. Her sample cases, however, were not returnable. After much thought about how best to utilize them, she contacted a local retirement home to offer a free demonstration without the end-of-party sales pitch. I was invited to help.

We arrived at the retirement home with two sample cases and a shopping bag full of washcloths, cotton balls, makeup mirrors, cotton swabs, and boxes of tissues. The activities director showed us to a recreation room conveniently equipped with a large round table, good lighting, and a functioning sink. We unpacked our supplies as aides went to bring our guests to the party.

One by one, five ladies were brought in and seated around the table. Three were wheelchair bound; two used walkers. All were white-haired, shriveled, hunched . . . mere skeletal beings. From seventy-nine to ninety-one years of age, the ladies greeted us pleasantly, and, with heads bowed and hands folded in laps, thanked us for giving them something different to do. They seemed *very* old, totally resigned to the blandness of themselves and their lives. My soul cringed.

I acted as assistant, handing out samples of cleansing cream, warm washcloths, and then moisturizers. The ladies remarked how pleasant the cream felt on their faces and how soft it left their skin. As they chatted, I realized they were not as drab and old on the inside as they were on the outside. That gave me an idea: Rather than consider them fragile grannies, I decided to relate to them as I would my own girlfriends.

Two were legally blind, and the others had minimal vision. We offered them the choice to forego the makeup demonstration. Without exception, they wanted the makeup and asked us to apply it. Happy to comply, my friend dabbed on face powder. I followed with an eyebrow pencil. As I stroked soft sienna where brows used to be, I raved about the women's radiantly glowing skin and teased about how sexy they would look after their "celebrity" makeovers.

"Who wants daytime eye shadow and who wants sultry, evening eyes?" I asked.

All hands went up for the sultry, sexy look! They were definitely getting into it, and I obliged with touches of brown shadow.

Finally, it was time for lipstick. Every head turned up, presenting dainty shrunken lips, to receive the muted red color. Those who still had vision wrestled with makeup mirrors, trying to see themselves. The activities director and aides "oohed" and "aahed" over how lovely the women looked. When I called them "gorgeous temptresses," each one sat a littler taller, beaming.

A camera appeared, courtesy of the activities director, and the ladies were thrilled to oblige, each requesting an

8 x 10! They had individual photos taken and then several group shots, to guarantee they'd come away with one photo good enough to be posted on the dining room bulletin board.

Watching the photo shoot, I thrilled at the transformation. Yes, the touches of makeup gave the women renewed color, but something else, something mystical, had happened. The "old ladies" were now animated, planning their lunchtime assault on the dining room, asking the aides to help them change into "prettier" dresses, joking about flirting with this or that man. I could not believe my eyes: The "old ladies" had become young women again—vibrant women—alive once more with the joy of their sexuality.

I suddenly realized I had not only been a witness to a miracle, but an instrument in its formation. Teary-eyed, I felt my heart pound with gratitude that I had been chosen to give those five women a spectacular gift at the end of their lives—the gift of feeling young again, even if only for an afternoon.

Lynne Daroff

In 2001, 37 percent of people aged sixty-five and older lived alone.

Find Simple Ways to Help People in Your Community

- Supervise children at community summer programs.
- Teach someone how to read.
- Form a neighborhood snow-shoveling group.
- Offer to drive children or elderly people to places they need to be.
- Train somebody to use a computer.
- Serve refreshments to runners at a local charity race.
- Tutor children.
- Teach ESL (English as a second language) to non-English speakers.
- Organize community barbeques, fun days for kids, bake-offs, contests, and gatherings.
- Direct a school play.
- Put in some time at a local soup kitchen.
- Design a visual arts class.
- Read to the ill or blind.
- Baby-sit for a parent in your community who needs an afternoon or evening off.
- Take part in adult literacy programs.
- Create a floral arrangement for a local seniors' center, nursing home, or hospital.
- Research local volunteer organizations and offer your assistance.

They Gave at the Office

We make a living by what we get.
We make a life by what we give.

WINSTON CHURCHILL

I t was the worst possible news: The doctors had found a malignant lump in her right breast, requiring an immediate lumpectomy. Cydel was only fifty-five years old. Her parents were in their eighties and took it very hard. Her two adult daughters were naturally very concerned, but it was winter and they lived out of town; the closest one, Julie, was some six hours away. Cydel's husband, Brian, took over most of the daily household chores, but between the doctor's appointments, mammograms, biopsies, and the surgery itself, the fight for her health took over Cydel's life.

Just two weeks after the surgery, she returned to her job as the secretary of administration to the sheriff of Ida County, Iowa. Cydel was one of "the new kids on the block," having worked only three years in a small office of sixteen people. Sitting at her desk, she wondered whether she could get through her workday and the chemotherapy and six weeks of radiation treatments that lay ahead. Cydel put in five- to six-hour workdays that first week, and the next week she was back to full time. Could she fight for her life and keep her job at the same time?

Italy has an average of 42 days of annual vacation, while France has 37, Germany has 35, Brazil has 34, Britain has 28, Canada has 26, Japan has 25, and the United States has a paltry 12.

Two months after returning to work, Cydel was busy at her desk when the chief deputy, Tom Peterson, called her into the deputy room, where he waited with Sheriff Wade Harriman and Deputy Kevin Frank. He nonchalantly handed her some paperwork. Scanning the internal office memo, Cydel first thought he was claiming compensation time for a vacation. But she burst into tears as she read the note.

The state of Iowa had allowed Cydel six weeks of vacation days and overtime to be used for her radiation treatments and recovery—donated by six of her coworkers.

Secretly, they had gone to their boss, Sheriff Harriman, and explained what they wanted to do. They had even called Thomas Miller, the Iowa attorney general in Des Moines, to secure permission to transfer their hard-earned hours to her record. This group of deputies was sacrificing their hours—vacation days and overtime—for her.

Dave was an investigator and a gentle giant. Mike, a shy, young fellow, had just joined the department and had been working there for only six months. Sheldon was always cracking jokes and talking trivia. Kevin was a murder and burglary investigator. Randy was one for telling a good animated story. Tom, the chief deputy, could talk to anyone and make them feel special.

In all, six deputies had given Cydel Maxwell one week each of their precious time. A grand total of 240 hours, some of which could have been paid out to them in cash. Without their help, Cydel would not have had enough time to cover her daily treatments, plus the two-hour roundtrip ride to Sioux City.

With excitement and relief, she tearfully accepted their generous offer. And all through the day, as the deputies returned to the office from their beats, Cydel thanked each of them individually for helping her do the impossible.

Six months later, after successfully finishing her treatments, Cydel invited the whole office over to her home for a backyard barbeque—to honor her special guests for their gift of life. Looking around at the six deputies that warm summer's day, Cydel smiled as she recalled Ida County's motto: "To Protect and Serve."

And how!

Bertamae Anger Ives

Brighten a Coworker's Day

- Pitch in and help with some unpleasant office tasks.

- Tell your colleagues how much you appreciate them.

- Invite someone new to lunch.

- When a coworker needs to talk, have lunch with him or her and listen with compassion.

- Walk an employee to a car or bus after hours.

- Drop off a treat at someone's desk or bring in a weekly treat that everyone can share.

- Offer to baby-sit a colleague's children so he or she can have an evening off.

- Remember employees' birthdays.

- Organize a regular potluck lunch.

- Invite a coworker's child to follow you around for a day and learn about your job.

- Do some yard work or cooking for a coworker who is ill or recovering from surgery.

- Teach one of your skills to a coworker and learn a skill from her.

- Give employees the option to take half a paid day to volunteer at a local charity of their choice. Help them research a charity that most interests them.

- Offer to switch a shift with a colleague who needs time off.

Mr. Roy

So many people say they want to save the world.
Just try your block, will you?

REV. CECIL WILLIAMS

Twenty years ago, we were desperate to move out of Detroit. The old Brightmore area had turned into a gathering place for motorcycle clubs. My husband, Mike, worked midnights, and I was home alone one night with our three young sons when seventeen gunshots erupted in an alley behind our house. We later learned the gangs were having a shoot-out from two bars at the end of our street. That was the last straw! The next day I started packing up boxes. I was determined to get out of this war zone.

> One of every four Americans moves each year—some 43 million people.

We began looking for houses in the Metro Detroit suburbs. House hunting is a discouraging task when you have no collateral. The rundown houses we could afford were mostly in rough, low-income neighborhoods. Mike was ready to give up our search, but we had an appointment to see one more house in Garden City. Ah, that sounded so beautiful to me: Garden City, like a safe haven for my family.

We pulled up to a house on Marquette Avenue and saw a neat white bungalow with black shutters. This house had just what we needed: fenced-in backyard, two-car garage, and four bedrooms.

As we were looking around the property, an old man from the blue house next door came up to my husband.

"Are you thinking about buying this house?" he asked.

"Yes, we're thinking about it," Mike answered.

"Well, let me show you something. You see that grass right there?" he asked, pointing to a stretch of lawn alongside his driveway. "That's my grass," he said sternly. "But," he continued, "it looks like it's in your yard, so you have to mow it!"

Mike started laughing and knew right away that he was going to like our new neighbor.

Things fell into place, and within weeks we were moving into our new home. One night I awoke, startled to hear loud bangs outside, but then I realized it was just firecrackers and not gunshots. I breathed a sigh of relief, knowing we were a part of a civilized neighborhood. I could rest assured that Ben, age two, Chris, age five, and Tim, age seven, were safe now.

Over the years our next-door neighbor, Mr. Roy Longman, became a dear friend. We tried to teach our boys to respect their elders, but he did not want them to call him "Mr. Longman." It sounded too stuffy for him.

"Call me Windy," he said. "That's what all the neighbors call me because I like to talk so much." Of course, we could not do that. So we compromised and called him "Mr. Roy." After that he insisted on addressing me as "Ma'am."

Mr. Roy was a retired truck driver and sometimes used coarse language, but he was always quick to apologize. Though a little rough around the edges, he had a heart of gold.

All the neighbors knew and loved Mr. Roy. Sometimes early in the morning he would go up to Dunkin' Donuts and treat the policemen when they got off their midnight shift. They all loved shooting the breeze with Windy.

When Mike's job required him to work long hours, it was Mr. Roy who had time to fix the boys' bikes. He taught them how to change their tires and keep their chains oiled. He had a swimming pool in his backyard and told our boys to come swim whenever they liked. It was like having a grandpa living next door!

Mr. Roy was our own neighborhood watch person. Every night about one o'clock in the morning he and his dog, Moose, would walk the streets, patrolling the neighborhood. Many times he would tell us the next day, "You left your lights on in the garage, so I turned them off for you." Or, "I found your garbage cans out in the streets, so I put them away." And, "Tell the boys to keep the gate closed or your dogs will get lost."

When our boys got old enough to get their driver's permits, he would offer to take them out to practice in his old green Jeep. If the boys got into trouble, he would show up at my doorstep on their behalf. "Don't be too hard on them, Ma'am," he'd say. "They're just youngsters and will soon grow out of this reckless stage."

On special occasions, like a birthday or graduation, Mr. Roy would pop over to our house with his Polaroid camera.

He would keep one photo for his scrapbook and then give one to us.

As he got into his late seventies, it was getting harder for Mr. Roy to care for his yard. One autumn when the leaves covered his lawn, our boys brought their girlfriends along, and we all went next door to clean up his double lot. After a great time frolicking in the leaves, we managed to fill up seventeen large lawn bags to finish the job. He was so grateful, but it was a small gesture to say "Thank you" for two decades of caring.

About two years ago, I mentioned to Mike that I had not seen Mr. Roy in a while. The last two times he had stopped by, he hadn't looked his usual dapper self. Razor stubble, bleary, pain-filled eyes, and a slow, uneven gait had replaced his friendly, outgoing manner and snappy sense of humor. I was worried that something was wrong.

In November we were told Mr. Roy had cancer, the fast-spreading kind. Family and friends gathered at his hospital bed. Each of our grown sons came by for a last visit. Mr. Roy's wife, Helen, told us how much Mr. Roy loved our boys; he had pictures of them in his scrapbook. "He cared for them like his own grandchildren," she said.

Our "Mr. Roy" died in December, and his wife moved in with her daughter. But every summer Mike still mows that stretch of lawn that belonged to the old man next door who welcomed us into his neighborhood.

Sandra J. Campbell

Be a Good Neighbor

- Offer to walk your neighbor's dog.

- Fix your neighbor's porch or floodlights if you notice them out.

- House-sit for your neighbors when they are out of town: Water their plants, look after their pets, and take in their newspapers and mail.

- Make some extra cookies in your next batch and bring them next door.

- Introduce yourself to new neighbors and give them your telephone number in case they need anything.

- Help your neighbors by carrying in groceries, raking leaves, and running errands.

- If you're handy, ask your neighbor if he needs any repairs done.

- Take a meal to your neighbor if he or she is sick.

- Shovel your neighbor's part of the sidewalk or mow her lawn.

- If your neighbor is usually rushing off in the morning, offer him a "sack breakfast" like yogurt, a bagel and juice, or a cup of fresh fruit.

- Call your neighbors once a week to see how they are doing.

Chapter 2

FIRST
RESPONSE

We all have the extraordinary coded within us—waiting to be released.

JEAN HOUSTON

First on the Scene

Actions and words are the windows
through which the heart is seen.

AMERICAN PROVERB

On June 7, 1998, Terri and her husband, Wallace, were heading north on I-5 near Tacoma, Washington, when they noticed the cars ahead of them swerving to avoid hitting something in the middle of the freeway. As their car approached the object, Terri and Wallace were horrified to discover that it was a small child.

Terri pulled onto the shoulder, and, while Wallace stopped the traffic, Terri rushed to the boy's side. She learned from his companions, who had just arrived at the scene, that he was just five years old, his name was Marquis, and he had accidentally fallen from a train trestle above the highway. She could tell that he had suffered a massive head injury, but the rest of his body appeared unharmed. Coincidentally, Terri had received her First Aid and CPR certification just one week earlier and was grateful to note how much of the course material she was able to recall.

She remembered that the most important thing to do was to keep the boy conscious, so she told him that it was all right to cry and that he would be fine as long as he continued crying. As they waited for help to arrive on the scene, Terri regularly monitored Marquis's vital signs while Marquis followed her directions and sobbed as hard as he could. Once the paramedics arrived, Terri watched them load the wailing boy into the ambulance and take him away. Then she went home and fell apart.

She felt sick worrying about Marquis. While at the scene, Terri had been so wrapped up in getting the boy into the ambulance that she hadn't even noticed which fire department had arrived. She had to know if he had survived, what hospital he had been taken to, everything. She called every fire department she could think of in the Tacoma area. Eventually, she got hold of the Lakewood Fire Department, who told her that the boy had survived the ride to the ER and had been admitted to the local children's hospital.

"He cried the entire way to the hospital," they said. "We've never seen anyone with such a severe head injury cry that hard. Because of your quick actions and care, we think he has an excellent chance at survival."

Terri phoned the hospital and was put through to Marquis's mother, who asked her to come to the ICU and sit with him. Terri arrived with flowers and a giant stuffed gorilla and soon learned that Marquis had undergone brain surgery but was stable. She spent the entire day, and a good portion of the next few days, at the hospital with the little boy and his family.

During their visits, Terri learned that Marquis's family was struggling financially, so she did her best to help them out. At first, her assistance consisted of toys and food, but once she discovered that the family would not be able to cover the medical costs, she set up a fund in the boy's name at a local bank. The Seattle/Tacoma NBC affiliate helped spread the word, and soon the community was involved in the effort to help the family. Clothing donations poured in, and a local physical therapist vowed to aid with the boy's recovery by offering his services free of charge.

Six days after the accident, Marquis was released from the hospital. Terri was invited to visit the family's home, where she discovered that Marquis's family had very little indeed. They didn't have any beds, and they had few clothes. Marquis had lost one of his shoes—the only pair he had—when he fell from the trestle. His parents couldn't pay their bills, and their phone had been shut off. The father had been holding down two jobs to support his family, but he'd lost both when he didn't report for work after his son's accident.

After seeing the family's situation firsthand, Terri wanted to do even more to help. She brought clothes for the entire family—mostly donations people asked her to deliver—and bought Marquis a new pair of shoes. One of her friends even wrote a personal check to the family's landlord to cover their rent for a month.

To express their gratitude, the boy's father gave Terri a candle his son had made for him in school. "This is the only thing I have of value," he said, "and I want you to have it."

Terri refused, but when Marquis's father insisted, she humbly accepted the family's gift, knowing all the love that had gone into making it and everything that it now had come to represent.

In November 1998, Terri flew to Spokane, Washington, to receive the Governor's Lifesaving Award, and she was also chosen for the American Red Cross Local Heroes Award. In accepting her awards, she emphasized the importance of being trained in First Aid and CPR.

"Chances are," she said, "if you ever use it, it'll be to save someone you love rather than a stranger."

Though in the case of Marquis, that little stranger turned out to be someone Terri has come to love.

Nicole Christie

CPR doubles a victim's chance of survival from cardiac arrest.

 Know What to Say in Medical Emergencies

The words that you say at the scene of a medical emergency can be as important as what you do.

- Let the person know that you are there to help and that he can trust you.

- Get him to agree to help himself and be helped.

- Don't overpromise. Keep it truthful and simple. Stay grounded in compassion.

- Connect with the other person. Be where she is so you can help lead her to comfort and safety. Sometimes just a gentle touch is enough.

- Get her attention *elsewhere;* for pain relief, take the focus off the injury.

- Get the person to actively participate in his own healing. Make him feel that there is something helpful he can do.

Read more about how you can positively affect a person in their time of need:

The Worst Is Over: What to Say When Every Moment Counts by Judith Acosta and Judith Simon Prager

 ## *Learn CPR*

Cardiopulmonary Resuscitation (CPR) consists of mouth-to-mouth respiration and chest compression. CPR allows oxygenated blood to circulate to vital organs such as the brain and heart. CPR can keep a person alive until more advanced procedures (such as defibrillation— an electric shock to the chest) can treat the cardiac arrest. Invented in 1960, CPR doubles a person's chance of survival from sudden cardiac arrest.

Find out where you can take CPR classes. As a start, check out the American Heart Association's Web site at www.americanheart.org for a list of classes and organizations in your area.

Three Easy Steps

1. CALL

   Check the victim for unresponsiveness. If there is no response, call 911 and return to the victim. In most locations, the emergency dispatcher can assist you with CPR instructions.

2. BLOW

Tilt the head back and listen for breathing. If the victim is not breathing normally, pinch nose and cover the mouth with yours and blow until you see the chest rise. Give two breaths. Each breath should take 2 seconds.

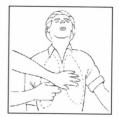

3. PUMP

If the victim is still not breathing normally, coughing, or moving, begin chest compressions. Push down on the chest 1½ to 2 inches fifteen times right between the nipples. Pump at the rate of 100 per minute, faster than once per second.

CONTINUE WITH 2 BREATHS AND 15 PUMPS UNTIL HELP ARRIVES.

NOTE: This ratio is the same for one-person and two-person CPR. In two-person CPR, the person pumping the chest stops while the other gives mouth-to-mouth breathing.

CPR for Children

CPR for children is similar to that for adults, but there are *four* essential differences:

1. If you are alone with the child, give one minute of CPR before calling 911.

2. Use the heel of one hand for chest compressions.

3. Press the sternum down 1 to 1½ inches.

4. Give one full breath followed by five chest compressions.

CPR for Infants

For babies less than one year of age:

1. Shout and gently tap the child on the shoulder. If there is no response, position the infant on his or her back.

2. Open the airway using a head–tilt lifting of chin. Do not tilt the head too far back.

3. If the baby is *not* breathing, give two small gentle breaths. Cover the baby's mouth and nose with your mouth. Each breath should be 1½ to 2 seconds long. You should see the baby's chest rise with each breath.

4. Give five gentle chest compressions at the rate of 100 per minute. Position your third and fourth fingers in the center of the chest, half an inch below the nipples. Press down only ½ to 1 inch.

5. Repeat with one breath and five compressions. After one minute of repeated cycles, call 911, and continue giving breaths and compressions.

Roadside Samaritan

What do we live for if it is not to make life less difficult for each other?

GEORGE ELIOT

We'd had a festive time at a reception on the West Side. At about 6:30 P.M., my friend Joyce and I were breezing along in the center of three lanes of heavy traffic, headed for home, when, without a burp or a gurgle, my faithful if elderly Chevy just stopped.

I fumbled and found the car's emergency flashers, and then, gingerly, slithered out between the rush of cars and tried to lift the hood, as one is supposed to do to signal trouble. Cars roared impatiently past me on both sides. The hood weighs a ton, and I was struggling to free the rod that would hold it up when a slim young man came up beside me, gently lowered the hood, and said, "Get in. I'll push you."

I had a quick glance at his dark face and backward base-ball cap and then glimpsed his sturdy-looking white pickup truck that had pulled up behind me. Visions of carjackings flashed through my mind—but he did have an honest face. Besides, I didn't have much choice.

"Slip it in neutral," he said, "and leave your flashers on." He spoke gently but firmly—as if he rescued older ladies stuck in the middle of a busy highway all the time.

I did as I was told. Getting past the whizzing line of cars on the outside lane was a bit tricky, but, with gentle bumps from my new friend, I managed to change lanes. Then, trying to turn, I realized that without power steering or power brakes, my turn would be far from graceful. My left front tire ended up halfway onto a strip of grass before I could stop.

> The American Automobile Association (AAA) receives nearly 30 million calls for emergency roadside assistance every year.

While I thanked my rescuer and told him that I would call the auto club, he pushed my car onto the pavement, turned to the back of his truck, and pulled out a hefty pair of jumper cables.

"I'm a mechanic," he explained with pride. After a few moments of trying to jump-start the old thing, the battery instrument panel showed only minimal response.

"I'm pretty sure it's the alternator," he said. *Whatever that was,* I thought, and said, "Oh dear, I'll call the auto club."

Joyce, with more time to look around, noticed that there was a young woman and a small boy sitting quietly in the cab of his car.

"Calling the auto club won't help," he said, still patiently. "A mile down this street is an auto parts store, where you can get an alternator."

"But I wouldn't know how to put it in!" I said.

His answer was softhearted, as if he were talking to his four-year-old son: "Turn off your lights, leave your emergency flashers on, and I will follow you there." His jumpers had injected just enough battery to drive that far, without lights. Meekly, I obeyed.

Once we were there, I went to the counter, where I bought the right alternator—a cubic foot of metal with lots of things sticking out of it. They told me that they would refund $40 of the $156 if I brought in the old one.

I asked my rescuer his name. "Robert" was all he volunteered as he picked up the old alternator and carried it back to the counter for a refund. Then he expertly installed the new alternator. I had no idea how to pay him. So I asked him his hourly rate. This would certainly count as overtime.

He grinned, shook his head, and said, "No charge."

Gratefully, I offered him some money, and Joyce did the same.

"To take your friends out to dinner," we insisted.

As we thanked him and shook hands, I hardly noticed his wings.

Marcia Reed

 ## *Know What to Do in Case of a Car Emergency*

- If you see someone who needs help, pull off the road and use your flashers to signal an emergency. Calmly tell the stranger you can help him, and you're not there to hurt him.

- Read your own car manual. Knowing the parts of your own car will help you assist someone else before a mechanic arrives.

- If the stranded motorists have children, make sure they are safe and warm. Make sure there are no scratches or bruises before you attend to the car.

- Check the oil and fluid. Check for tire damage. Try to start the car. Use your jumper cables if necessary. See if you can detect a potential problem. Are there leaks? Do you see dents, holes, or scratches in the engine? Is the battery dead? Is there enough oil? Enough fuel?

- Learn how to change a tire if you don't already know how.

Learn Emergency Driving Techniques

Brake Failure

- You can slow the vehicle down by shifting into a lower gear, releasing the clutch pedal (for manual transmissions), and applying the emergency brake.

- If the car is equipped with automatic transmission, apply the emergency brake and move the gear control lever into the low-range position. This could cause damage to the emergency brake and the transmission, but under the circumstances of brake failure there is no better choice.

Wet Brakes

- You can help dry the brakes by driving a short distance and applying light pressure to the brake pedal. The heat generated by the friction of the brakes against the brake drum will evaporate the water from the brake linings.

Stuck Gas Pedal

- Tap the gas pedal to try to unstick the throttle linkage or lift the pedal with your foot.

- Shift to neutral and apply firm pressure to the brakes without locking the wheels.

- Find a safe place to move the vehicle completely off the road.

Tire Blowout

- Hold the steering wheel tightly and try to keep the car straight on your side of the road.
- Reduce speed.
- Do not apply the brakes until the engine has slowed the car to allow you to maintain control of the vehicle.
- Find a safe place to move the vehicle completely off the road.
- If you begin to feel a bumpy ride when there is no obvious reason, stop and check your tires. You can tell a blowout by a loud noise and by the way the car begins to swerve.

Vehicle Approaching Head-On into the Path of Your Vehicle

- Reduce speed immediately.
- Sound your horn.
- Keep to the right even if this means running off the road.
- Tips to follow if you run off the pavement and onto the shoulder:

- Do not immediately apply the brakes or try to turn back; you could skid, lose control, or overturn.
- Slowly remove your foot from the accelerator and steer straight ahead.
- Allow the engine to slow the vehicle.
- When the car is stopped or nearly stopped, check for approaching traffic and if it's safe, gradually drive back onto the road.

 ### *Keep an Emergency Safety Kit in Your Car*

Include the following:

- Ice scraper and snow brush
- Flashlight with extra batteries
- Empty coffee can with candles and matches (for warmth)
- Sleeping bag or blankets (also for warmth)
- Reflective emergency blinker
- Bright tie that can be attached to an antenna
- Small shovel
- Rain gear and extra clothes such as mittens, socks, and a warm cap
- Bag of sand, cat box litter, or traction mats (in case you get stuck)

- Tow rope or cables
- Pair of jumper cables
- Basic first aid kit
- Small tools (including a screwdriver, pair of pliers, hammer, wrenches, and pocket knife)
- Nonperishable food (such as cereal bars or a jar of peanut butter and some crackers)
- Also a good idea: drinking water and easy-to-open canned fruit or vegetable juices to quench thirst

Daring Rescue

Life only demands from you the strength you possess.
DAG HAMMARSKÖLD

Angela Floda and her sister, Stacy Clements, were on their way to their mom's house in Warrington, Florida, with a carful of five kids—and two more on the way. Stacy was four months pregnant, and she'd just learned she was carrying twins.

"I can hardly wait," she told Angela—and it was at that very moment the two women first spotted the rising cloud of smoke.

"Is someone burning trash?" Angela wondered aloud, but as they rounded the corner the sisters discovered the real reason for the rapidly darkening skies.

"Oh dear God!" Stacy exclaimed, pointing to a house that was barely visible through a raging wall of flames.

"We've got to get help!" Angela cried out, screeching to a stop and throwing open her car door. "You kids stay right here," she cautioned her three children and Stacy's two, and together the sisters ran to a neighbor's and told him to call 911.

By now the front and entire right side of the house were completely engulfed in flames. About the only part of the single-story structure still untouched was the wheelchair ramp near a left side door.

"That's Mr. Tucker's place!" Angela remembered with a gasp, and without a second's hesitation she darted toward the burning house.

"Wait for me!" Stacy called, sprinting after her.

The house belonged to William Tucker, a widow in his eighties who had resided in the small, western Florida community for decades. As children, Angela and Stacy had waved to him countless times from their bikes while he gardened in his front yard. But then one day a stroke had left Tucker paralyzed.

"He'll never make it until the fire department gets here!" Angela worried as she vaulted the ramp railing and grabbed the doorknob. Fortunately, the door was unlocked, and it led directly into Tucker's bedroom.

Stacy shuddered with fear when her sister pushed open the door and disappeared inside. "I can't let her go in there alone!" she thought, and despite her condition Stacy followed her younger sister into the inferno.

The room was so smoke-filled the sisters could barely see their old friend and neighbor stretched out on his bed. "Mr. Tucker! You've got to wake up!" they shouted, but the elderly invalid was all but unconscious from smoke inhalation.

Tucker was too heavy for the sisters to carry to safety, but his wheelchair was beside the bed, and as the room grew hot as an oven they tugged and lifted and finally wrestled him into it.

The far bedroom wall burst into flames as Stacy pushed the chair toward the door. But on a shelf near the door Angela spotted Tucker's service commendations and a framed photograph of his wife. *I can save these, at least,* she thought and gathered them into her arms.

Outside, Angela and Stacy breathed deep lungsful of fresh

air. But they weren't out of danger yet. An RV was parked near the house—and the fire had nearly reached the propane tank.

"We've got to get further away!" Stacy exclaimed, and while Angela pushed Mr. Tucker toward their mom's house, Stacy jumped into the car and drove alongside. Seconds later the propane tank exploded in a fireball. But everyone was safe—thanks to Angela and Stacy.

Firefighters were amazed when they reached the scene a few minutes later. "He never would have survived without your help," the volunteer fire chief told the sisters. "You saved his life."

Mr. Tucker was treated for smoke inhalation. His house was completely destroyed by the fire, but today he's living an active life in a local retirement home.

"Thank you," he told Stacy and Angela, when they handed him the photographs and other mementoes Angela had rescued from the blaze.

"We'd do it again in a heartbeat," replied Stacy.

But Mr. Tucker didn't hear her gentle words. He was staring tearfully at the picture of his wife, grateful for the opportunity to see her smile and the faces of the two women who had given him the chance.

Heather Black

More than 80 percent of the deaths and 72 percent of the injuries in the United States occur in residential fires. The United States of America holds the worst fire record in the industrialized world.

 Practice Fire Prevention

Regularly check smoke detectors.

- It is recommended that you do this once every six months.
- Remind your neighbors to check their smoke detectors as well.

Prepare a fire escape plan.

- Make sure every member of your family knows of your plan and what he or she are to do should a fire occur. If possible, every room should have two escape routes.
- Special emphasis and instruction should be given to children so they fully understand what they are to do during a fire. Children are often concerned about the safety of their pets, so discuss this issue before a fire starts. In many cases, pets are able to get out on their own.
- Conduct fire drills so each member of the family can demonstrate what he or she must do during a fire.

- Make sure your escape route permits the safe exiting of the building should the main thoroughfare exits or doors be blocked during the fire.

- All windows that will be used to escape from the fire should be easily opened (from the inside).

- Have adequate ladders or fire escape mechanisms, should it be necessary to escape from upper levels of the building.

- Make sure everyone is familiar with how to use such equipment and that it is well maintained and tested before actual use.

- Encourage friends and neighbors to do the same. Ensure that your office also has a proper fire escape plan.

 Remember

If you see a fire or smoke coming from any structure, building, or area, or hear a smoke detector or fire alarm:

- *Immediately* call 911 to report what you see or hear *and* the location of the fire.

- If someone is trapped in the building, advise 911 of that fact and of the person's location in the building.

- Meet and tell the firefighters where the fire is. They can waste valuable minutes if they have to find it themselves.

- Everyone is responsible for preventing fires. But everyone is not obligated to fight major fires. In general, never join in the firefighting unless the firefighters request your help.

Should you know that someone is in a burning building and you want to rescue them, before you attempt to do so:

- Think before you act!
- Realize your limitations and the dangers involved. You could lose your own life, or be painfully burned or disabled. Also, you could easily be trapped in the fire yourself.
- Your attempted rescue could only make matters worse for everyone involved. A firefighter's life might also be on the line.

 Other Things You Can Do to Help

- If someone or their clothing is on fire, do not let her run—that will only fan the flames with more oxygen. If water is available, douse the flames. If not, roll the person in a blanket or coat on the ground to smother the flames.
- Offer a stuffed animal to help calm a hysterical child.
- If a neighbor's home is damaged by fire, offer to let him stay at your place—it's closer and friendlier than being in a hotel.

Chapter 3

THROUGH the EYES of a CHILD

> *No one has yet fully realized the wealth of sympathy, kindness, and generosity hidden in the soul of a child. The effort of every true education should be to unlock that treasure.*
>
> EMMA GOLDMAN

Gopher Tails and Ice Cream

*We are used to thinking in terms of what
we can teach our children.
Maybe we need to ask ourselves what
we may learn from them.*

PIERO FERRUCCI

"Two scoops please, Mr. Mason." Reggie's missing front teeth adds a lisp to his words. He counts his five pennies onto the drugstore counter. He had clutched the pennies so tightly the four blocks from home that their circle imprints held the metallic scent on the palm of his hand.

"I know, I know." Mr. Mason punches the 5-cent key, tosses the pennies into the till, and slams it closed. "It's the same every Saturday night, isn't it? One scoop strawberry with one scoop maple nut on top."

The ceiling fan overhead barely turns the humid August air. The wood floorboards squeak under Reggie's shifting feet. He knows there is no way to hurry Mr. Mason through his weekly lecture. Reggie waits respectfully, as his mother would want him to.

"You children these days. As if these times aren't hard enough!" Mr. Mason dishes out his criticism with the cone. "Your father hurt in the mine cave-in and your mama not well. This ice cream will be gone in minutes. You could have bought something useful, something to help out your mama."

"Yes, Mr. Mason," Reggie nods without really hearing. His focus is on the nearly-ready-to-drip ice cream.

Mr. Mason finally hands the cone to him. "After all, your family works hard for what little they have, every penny of it."

"Yes, Mr. Mason," Reggie agrees before taking the cone and hurrying home.

Reggie knows that Mr. Mason is right. His family does work hard for every penny they earn. All families do. "It's hard times," the adults say to each other.

Reggie wanted to help his family. He was the youngest of nine, and it was hard to watch his older brothers and sisters all working, but seven years old is too young to go down into the mines with his brothers. So, when the posters went up all over town explaining that the gophers were ruining what scanty crop there was and offering to pay a penny a gopher tail, Reggie was excited that he had finally found a way to earn some money.

Every day, after hauling water, feeding the chickens and gathering their eggs, hoeing in the acre garden and helping his mother gather the ripened vegetables, Reggie would grab some bread and cheese and a jar of water and set off into the prairie scrub to catch gophers.

The sun was at its highest and hottest, and the prairie wind kicked up the dust from the dry ground. The grasshoppers raised out of the fields one jump ahead of his every step.

Lying in the sticker grass, Reggie would wait patiently for the gophers to come out of their holes. All day he caught gophers, and every Saturday morning he would proudly turn over his money to Mama, all except five pennies.

"Bless you, Reggie," his mother smiled down at him as the coins clanked into the baking powder tin she used for savings.

Reggie would smile back while making a fist around the five pennies he kept deep in his pocket for this Saturday night's treat. Reggie runs up the pebble walk and slams through the front screen door of home. His lungs work to suck in the summer thick air. He heads straight back to the bedroom where he can finally savor the prize of his hard work. The maple nut has dripped down with a hint of strawberry showing through, but he had made it home without losing any of the cone.

"Reggie." His mama opens her eyes and pulls herself up in bed. "Oh, Reggie, again you bring me ice cream!"

The dripping cone leaves no time for arguing over who should eat it. His mother takes the cone and pats the bed for him to sit next to her.

Reggie climbs up and snuggles into her.

"My favorite flavors. You always remember." His mother's love floods through him.

"I'll always remember, Mama," he said.

And even these sixty years later, he always has.

Cynthia M. Hamond

Top Ten Ice Cream–Consuming Countries in the World

1. United States
2. New Zealand
3. Denmark
4. Australia
5. Belgium / Luxembourg
6. Sweden
7. Canada
8. Norway
9. Ireland
10. Switzerland

 How Kids Can Help Family and Friends

- Help your parents, grandparents, or family friends with yard work: Help them weed their gardens, water their plants, or mow their lawns.
- Pick fresh flowers and leave them on the doorstep of a friend.
- Tutor an older relative or friend in computer skills.
- Call or e-mail a sick relative.

- Design a cookbook of treasured family recipes and get your family and friends together to cook up some of the delicacies.

- Assemble a birthday chart of your immediate and more distant family members and call them on their birthdays.

- Use a video camera to interview your grandparents about their childhoods and make a keepsake copy of the video for them.

- Learn how to play an instrument and put on a concert for your friends and relatives.

- Create an art project as a surprise gift for your aunt or uncle, or make a frame, put a meaningful photo in it, and present it to them.

- Write something about a family member or friend: a poem, song, or biographical sketch.

- Organize family photos and compile them in a scrapbook for your parents or grandparents. Fill it with mementos and memories. Create a personalized, heartfelt card expressing how much you appreciate them.

The Blue Angora Hat

*Parents can only give good advice or put
them on the right paths, but the
final forming of a person's character
lies in their own hands.*

ANNE FRANK

I must have been about twelve that December. We had
already had a fair amount of snow, and the tempera-
tures stayed in the low teens. By Swedish standards,
however, winter had hardly begun.

The remote village where I lived had a very small school.
Any education beyond fourth grade meant either being
boarded with another family or a daily train ride of two
hours each way.

I rode the train. The passenger cars were well heated, and
that morning I reluctantly removed my blue angora hat and
placed it on my lap. Angora hats were the "in" thing that
year, and for weeks I had been the only girl in my class who
didn't have one.

The angora goat, an enchanting animal, is one of the oldest
surviving animals known to man and is said to have origi-
nated in the mountains of Tibet, homeland of the pious Tibetan
monk.

My parents were trying hard to make ends meet while raising five children. Since I already had a hat, I knew better than to ask for another one. And then, one day, my mother handed me a package. It was really a Christmas present, she explained, but with the weather already being so cold, she decided to give it to me before the holidays. The angora hat was everything my heart had desired. At that moment I didn't care if it was the only present I'd get that year.

The train had stopped. When the doors opened, I looked up from my history book and watched the new passengers embark. As they slowly proceeded down the aisle, I realized with dismay who they were. They were all patients from the institution.

Right above the train depot, surrounded by woods and fields, stood a large brick building. It was a home for the mentally retarded. Occasionally, as the train passed by, the patients would wave, and sometimes we waved back. Then, invariably, someone would make a snide remark.

A short, slender woman, obviously the nurse in charge of the group, now steered one of her patients over to the seat across from mine. Then the nurse left.

Uneasily, I resumed my studying while furtively watching my new companion. She was dressed in a brown shapeless coat that was much too large, almost reaching her ankles. Her head was covered by a wool scarf that was tied under her chin. Although she was looking out the window, her eyes did not seem to focus on anything in particular, and her face was without expression.

For a while I kept an eye on her, but she seemed harmless enough. Soon I turned my attention back to my homework. I had some math to do, and I moved the angora hat from my lap to make room for my notebook.

I didn't see her get up, but suddenly she was sitting next to me. Clutching my books, I instinctively moved closer to the window. Then I saw why she had moved. She had seen my hat. Her hand was gently stroking the soft, feathery yarn.

My first reaction was to yank it away from her—how dare she touch my most precious possession?—but then I stopped myself.

There was something in the way she was looking at the hat that suddenly touched my heart. It was the hunger for something unattainable, a desire for what you could not have—and oh, how I could identify with that feeling.

Noticing my stare, she focused her eyes on my hat. Smiling gently, she said, "Nice. Nice hat."

"Yes," I said somewhat reluctantly. "It's nice. Blue is my favorite color."

Unexpectedly, the nurse appeared. She took her patient by the arm and guided her back to her seat.

A look of bewilderment came over the woman's face, as if she had been scolded for something that she didn't understand.

Now I put my hat on. "Do you like it?" I asked.

Her smile returning, she nodded vigorously.

My heart warmed toward her. "It was supposed to be a Christmas present," I confided, "but I got it early. . . ."

I wasn't sure whether she understood, but again she nodded.

"Would you like to try it on?"

Now the smile vanished, and she looked uncertainly at

me. It came as a shock to realize that she was a young woman. Somehow, because of the way she was dressed, she had looked like an old lady.

I held out the hat while indicating that she needed to remove her scarf.

The transformation was miraculous. The hat made her look almost beautiful. The color brought out the blue of her eyes and made her face glow.

I jumped up from my seat. "Come on," I cried. "Let's go and look in the mirror."

She took my hand as trustingly as a child, and we walked over to the narrow mirror at the end of the aisle. Hand in hand we stood there, a skinny girl with blond pigtails and freckles and a young woman with straight hair and rosy cheeks wearing a pale blue angora hat.

Our eyes met in the mirror, and for a brief moment we were sisters, sharing the pleasure of something beautiful that transcends all ages and all mental limitations.

"What is your name?" I asked my newfound friend. "Mine is Elisabet."

But before she had a chance to reply, the nurse was there. She gave me a friendly nod. "This is where we get off," she said. "It was nice of you to talk to Anna. You'd better take your hat back."

She reached out to get it, but I put my hand on her arm.

"No," I said. That I would be the only girl in class again without an angora hat suddenly seemed unimportant. "No, I don't want it back. I have another one at home."

The nurse looked doubtful. "Are you sure you want to give it away?" she asked.

"Yes," I said. "Yes, I'm sure."

I discovered I was still holding Anna's hand. Now I moved it up to touch the hat.

"For you," I said. "A Christmas present."

As they stepped off the train, I rolled down the window and leaned out.

"Good-bye, Anna," I cried. "Good-bye." I waved at her and she waved back.

The train started moving. Soon Anna was only a blue dot in the distance—and then she was gone.

Elisabet McHugh

 Teach Children about Giving

- Encourage your kids to help care for an ailing friend or neighbor, a household pet, or a young plant or tree.

- When your child does something altruistic, let him know that you value his generosity to others as much as you value his achievements at school or on the sports field.

- Volunteering can be a lot of fun for a child. To start, look for a cause that involves your child's interests or talents. For example, if she is interested in baseball, she could take time to help to clean up the diamond. If he is good at art, he could find a preschool program that needs help supervising the youngsters.

Most schools and churches, and many communities, have volunteer groups for kids.

- Set a shining example. Look after an elderly neighbor, serve dinner at a local woman's shelter, or help out at a fund-raising run for your favorite charity. Invite your children to come along, and ask them for ways they think they can really help out and be of service.

- Make it part of your daily routine to look out for opportunities to do good for people you know and love and for people you haven't yet met. When you're shopping at the grocery store, see how many doors you can open for others, especially for senior citizens or people with extra needs.

- Try to get your child's school to initiate projects that teach kids to assist others. A child care center can collect blankets to donate to shelters. An elementary class can collect toys for other children in need. A shop class can build furniture for low-income families.

Things Kids Have Done to Make a Difference

- Twelve-year-olds in Sandwich, Massachusetts, testified at their state capitol to help pass a law that would ban smoking on public school grounds. The law was passed, and several other states adopted similar laws.

- In Chelmsford, Massachusetts, a twelve-year-old started a petition and testified with friends at a town meeting to protect a wooded area from being destroyed by a condominium development project. The woods are still there.

- A Chicago community health clinic that provides services for poor, pregnant women and infants was about to be shut down for lack of funds. Fifty children organized a protest in front of the clinic, drawing the attention of the media and lawmakers. The clinic remained open.

- Fourth-grade students in Kittery, Maine, ran a canned food drive at their school and donated the food to the local food pantry. Representatives of the classes helped prepare the food for distribution to the clients of the food pantry.

- Students from the sixth grade at a private school in New York City gave up a weekend to help raise funds for World Hunger Year. Some of them were on the phone bank during the annual HUNGERTHON radio show.

A Great Big Hug

We can do no great things—
only small things with great love.

MOTHER TERESA

Four-year-old Matthew was a little boy wise beyond his years. When he was brought to our children's wish foundation by his mother, he was already suffering from the advanced stages of AIDS. Despite his illness, he possessed a maturity and strong will that were unique and unusual for such a young child.

One of his favorite pastimes was looking at all the photographs that hung on our walls, pictures of children enjoying their wish trips. He would spend long periods of time observing the many images of smiles, laughter, and memories.

Late one afternoon, Matthew had the opportunity to meet a wish mother, a woman who had lost her daughter Elisha suddenly the previous summer to a rare infection. Earlier that day, Matthew had been admiring a picture taken during her wish trip, so I felt that he would be happy to meet her mother.

"Matthew, this is Elisha's mom."

Looking up at the two of us, he immediately focused on her with curiosity and interest.

"Is Elisha still alive?" he asked without hesitation.

"No," she replied, as she softly shook her head from side to side.

"Do you miss her?" His face twisted into a look of concern and understanding.

His innocent persistence seemed to touch the woman rather than irritate her, as she answered simply, "Very much so."

She turned to walk away, but Matthew called after her. "I'm going on a trip to heaven soon. If you want to, you can give me a hug and I can bring it to Elisha."

Her heart filled with tears, Elisha's mom knelt down, gathered Matthew into her arms, and gave him a great big hug. After they parted, Matthew ran off to look at more pictures, having no idea what had just transpired.

A month later, Matthew passed away. I decided to call Elisha's mother to let her know. We spoke about him for quite a while, remembering his enthusiasm and genuine spirit.

She explained that Matthew had played a significant role in her healing process. This messenger of love had given her the only thing she really needed—the chance to finally say good-bye to her little girl.

Laura Hogg

Twenty-two million people have died of AIDS worldwide, including more than 3 million last year. That is more than 8,000 per day—or nearly six deaths every minute.

Find Out More about Children's Wish-Granting Organizations

- Make-A-Wish Foundation: www.wish.org

  The Make-A-Wish Foundation grants wishes to children under the age of eighteen with life-threatening illnesses. It is the largest wish-granting organization in the world, with eighty chapters in the United Stated and its territories and twenty international affiliates.

- A Special Wish Foundation: www.spwish.org

  A Special Wish Foundation, Inc., is a nonprofit charitable organization dedicated to granting the wishes of children under the age of twenty-one who have been diagnosed with a life-threatening disorder. Founded in 1982, A Special Wish Foundation was one of the first wish-granting organizations in the United States, and now has chapters across the United States and one in Moscow, Russia.

- The Grant-A-Wish Foundation: www.grant-a-wish.org

  Grant-A-Wish is a national children's charity that provides educational, recreational, and supportive services to children eighteen and under who are battling life-threatening illnesses. They offer services that provide comfort and hope to kids suffering from cancer, leukemia, cystic fibrosis, neurological diseases, and various other critical illnesses. In addition to wish granting, they also offer eight additional programs, including support group sponsorship and hospital housing, that provide support to critically ill children and their families throughout the treatment process.

- The Starlight Children's Foundation: www.starlight.org

    Starlight Children's Foundation's focus is to lift the spirits of seriously ill kids and their families at times of great stress and hardship. Services are provided for seriously, chronically, and terminally ill children, aged four through eighteen years. Programs are administered and wishes granted throughout the fifty states and internationally through local chapters.

Donate Your Airline Miles to Fly a Terminally Ill Child on Their Dream Trip

Most airlines offer ways to donate your miles to a charity so that it can fulfill a child's wish. Contact the particular wish-granting organization for more specifics on how this can be done.

The Umbrella

It is in the shelter of each other that the people live.

IRISH PROVERB

We had moved to India for two years, and soon after our arrival, New Delhi was experiencing its hardest monsoon rains of the year.

In the middle of the afternoon, I discovered that my youngest son, Jimmy, who was only nine at the time, had taken our oversized black umbrella and had gone out for a walk. I was very worried about him, as the streets were so flooded.

When he came in an hour later, he was soaked to the bone.

"Where have you been?" I asked, relieved and irritated.

He told me that he had walked down to the *nullah,* an open drain by the bridge near our home.

"You know that man who sells corn over there?" he started off.

"Yes?" I replied anxiously, awaiting his explanation.

"Well," he continued, "he's got a son—he's about my age. He was sitting all huddled up and his fire had gone out. So I sat down beside him and we both got under the umbrella and sat there. Then his father and his mother and his little brother came. His mother was the most pregnantest lady I ever saw. His little brother didn't have anything on, and he got under the umbrella too. And they were all shivering so hard and I wasn't."

He paused to think before he added. "And then they all went away so I came home." He smiled and then headed off to play in his room.

I stood there for a moment with nothing but the pounding rains above, staring at the umbrella dripping on the floor, and grateful for my child's open heart and for the roof over our heads.

Betty Ann Webster

A quarter of the world's population—1.3 billion people—live in severe poverty. In industrialized countries, more than 100 million people live below the poverty line, more than 5 million people are homeless, and 37 million are jobless.

 ## *Make a Difference in the Lives of the Homeless*

- Donate food to local shelters. They especially need items like juice, meats, soups, and stews. Take along some freshly baked items. Load up a bag full of non-perishable groceries and donate it to a food drive in your area. If your community doesn't have a food drive, organize one. Contact your local soup kitchens, shelters, and homeless societies and ask what kind of food items they would like.

- Instead of handing out money, buy the food yourself, refer the person to an agency that can provide
  food, shelter, and other assistance, or give coupons to
  restaurants or grocery stores that can be turned in
  for food.

- Donate clothes such as jackets, sweatshirts, new
  underwear, socks, shoes, knit hats, and gloves that are
  needed for men and women.

- Because the fastest growing groups of homeless
  people are children and women with children, there
  is a need for disposable diapers, baby food and for-
  mula, clothing, and blankets.

- Tutor homeless children. A tutor can make all the
  difference. Just having adult attention can spur children to do their best. Many programs in shelters,
  transitional housing programs, and schools require
  interested volunteers. Or begin you own tutoring
  volunteer corps at your local shelter. It takes nothing
  more than a little time.

- In communities where there is a "bottle recycling
  law," collecting recyclable cans and bottles is often
  the only "job" available to the homeless. But it is an
  honest job that requires initiative. You can help by
  saving your recyclable bottles, cans, and newspapers
  and giving them to the homeless instead of taking
  them to a recycling center or leaving them out for
  collection. If you live in a larger city, you may wish
  to leave your recyclables outside for the homeless to

pick up—or give a bagful of cans to a homeless person in your neighborhood.

- Volunteer your professional talents. No matter what you do for a living, you can help the homeless with your on-the-job talents and skills. People with clerical skills can train others with little skills. Doctors, psychiatrists, counselors, and dentists can treat the homeless in clinics. Lawyers can help with legal concerns. Homeless people's needs are bountiful— your time and talent won't be wasted.

- Volunteer your hobbies. Every one of us has something we can give the homeless. Wherever our interests may lie—cooking, repairing, gardening, photography—we can use them for the homeless. Through our hobbies, we can teach them useful skills, introduce them to new avocations, and perhaps point them in a new direction.

- Taking time to talk to a homeless person in a friendly, respectful manner can give them a wonderful sense of civility and dignity. And besides being just neighborly, it gives the person a weapon to fight the isolation, depression, and paranoia that many homeless people face.

- Recognize that the homeless are as diverse as the colors of a rainbow. The person you meet may be a battered woman, an addicted veteran, someone who is lacking job skills . . . the list goes on.

What Children Can Do for the Homeless

- Take homeless children on trips with your kids. Frequently, the only environment a homeless child knows is that of the street, shelters, or other transitory housing. Outside of school—if they attend—these children have little exposure to many of the simple pleasures that most kids have. Volunteer at your local family shelter to take children skating or to an aquarium on the weekend.

- Have your children clean out their closets and give some of their old clothes to homeless children, or take your kids and buy some new clothing for the homeless, especially socks and underwear.

- Give toys. Homeless children dream of new toys such as dolls, trucks, and games. These donations may be the only gifts they receive for a birthday or the holidays. Homeless parents have more urgent demands on what little money they have, such as food and clothing. So often these children have nothing to play with and little to occupy their time. You can donate toys, books, and games to family shelters to distribute to homeless children. For Christmas or Chanukah, ask your friends and coworkers, and their children, to buy and wrap gifts for homeless children.

- Play with children in a shelter. Many children in shelters are cut off from others their own age.

Shuffled from place to place, sometimes these kids don't attend school on a regular basis and have no contact with other kids. Bring a little joy to their lives by taking your children to a local shelter to play. Plan activities such as coloring, playing with dolls, or building model cars (bring along whatever toys you'll need). Take a few extra sandwiches when you go.

- Help your children's class organize a classroom drive or a schoolwide drive collecting caps, hats, socks, and mittens and other winter items to donate to a homeless shelter. Have teachers collect donations and design flyers, letters to parents, and posters to make announcements for classrooms.

 Things Kids Have Done to Help the Homeless

- A group of preschool kids helped their mothers plan and serve a meal at a homeless shelter.
- An elementary school class made "Share Care Bags," with soap, shampoo, combs, and toothbrushes for a women's shelter. They even enclosed personal notes!
- A Sunday School group collected toys, games, and sports equipment and gave them to children at a homeless center.
- A group of fifth graders had a holiday party for homeless children.

Coach Brock

Flatter me, and I may not believe you.
Criticize me, and I may not like you.
Ignore me, and I may not forgive you.
Encourage me, and I will not forget you.

WILLIAM ARTHUR WARD

Every now and then, you come across a coach who does more than teach a child how to bat and catch and slide into home plate. We've had a long success record with all three of my sons and their volunteer coaches. The fathers and some mothers who work long hours, put out numerous fires on the job, and still make coaching baseball to kids a priority all deserve recognition. My hat is off to every one of you.

But one coach in particular stands out. My youngest, Mikey, just finished up a season under Coach Brock. Mikey didn't get a hit for maybe ten or twelve games. Week after week, he'd walk back to the dugout after striking out, his head hung so low the brim of his cap covered his whole face. More than once he made the third out, ending the inning, and the outfield all rushed in, leaping into the air and throwing up their gloves, a contrast to my little batter walking back to the dugout in utter defeat.

It was clear he felt the weight of not only failing himself when it was time to perform but, worse, failing the team.

There was no apparent frustration on the part of our coach with the inevitable out my son made. Although I am sure he wanted to win, Coach Brock went out of his way to encourage my son after each and every out. He leaned down toward Mikey, stopping him on his long walk back to the team, and put both of his hands on my son's shoulders. I never heard what his coach said to him, but I could tell by the way my son slowly raised his head to meet his coach's eyes that his words were heartening.

These words that this coach spoke to my son at his lowest moments made all the difference. They made the difference between completely losing interest in the game and coming doggedly to every practice, intent on improvement. Not one time did I sense anything but sheer excitement about playing baseball from this child, despite his failure to make contact with the ball. Never did he act dejected or inadequate about being the only one in the entire league not to make any contact whatsoever with the ball. By mid-season, even a foul tip would have been considered a success in my book.

The only comments Mikey made about any game were about plays he almost made in the field. I know this kind of positive mentality did not come from the mind of an eight-year-old. They were planted there by his coach.

And Mikey absorbed the coach's words as well as his actions. The pizza the coach made good on after his first hit, the extra hours the coach practiced with him, and the continuous positive feedback all made this season, the season of rarely coming through home base, probably one of the greatest seasons in sports my son will ever have.

I missed the game that mattered most to my son. But the game ball never left his hands for days and now sits in a place of honor in our house. Who would think a grimy, used baseball could take on a persona? But this one did.

That ball shouts to my son. *"Keep trying!"* and *"You can do it!"* and other things only he can hear. There were other players who, play for play, deserved that ball far more than my son. But this coach knew who needed it the most.

"He has given me hope," Mikey said earnestly of his hero.

And that is the beginning of all sorts of possibilities.

Ferris Robinson

Little League baseball has become the world's largest organized youth sports program. In the space of just six decades, Little League grew from three teams to nearly 200,000 teams, in all fifty U.S. states and more than 100 countries.

Be a Good Volunteer Coach

Being a good volunteer coach involves many complicated aspects influencing a young person's life. Of course you'll need the basic equipment for your sport, but you also need the right skills, attitudes, and values:

- You have basic organizational skills.

- You have a little bit of disposable income, because it will cost you some amount of money to care.

- You should have a good sense of humor, because coaching is fun!

- You can motivate, teach, and be a role model for your players.

- You demonstrate and communicate a good sense of values: fair play, sportsmanship, respect, and team-work.

- You have a positive attitude.

- You enjoy working with children and are not easily frustrated by them.

- You have good communication skills with both kids and parents.

- You are safety-conscious and have basic first aid skills or knowledge.

- You have knowledge of the sport you are coaching, or you are willing to learn.

Grandpa's Love

*In every child who is born, under no circumstances,
and of no matter what parents, the potentiality
of the human race is born again.*

JAMES AGEE

"Grandpa! Grandpa! Can you come to school to see the baby chicks?"

Daniel was in first grade. He had talked about the baby chicks all weekend.

Due to be out the door in ten seconds, my not-dressed-and-ready-for-the-day father was left laughing and anxious by this request. It was Monday morning, and we had to be out the door immediately to get Daniel to school on time. After deliberating over his unshaved whiskers and mismatched attire, my father declared, as only a grandpa could, "Why sure! I wouldn't miss it for the world!"

My mom and dad were visiting for the weekend to meet our newest child—this delightful, spunky, front-teeth-missing little boy. As a foster child, Daniel was in need of a safe and loving place to live while his mom tried to piece together a life scarred by poor choices. Daniel was the second child to be placed in our home (and our hearts), and it was his fourth placement in eighteen months. To Daniel, we were Brenda and Tim, but almost instantly my parents were given the grand and glorious titles of Grandma and Grandpa. He won their hearts as quickly as they won his.

Curled up on my mom's lap the second night of their visit, Daniel was quizzing her on why she had "extra skin" on her face. I left the room giggling as I heard her wryly explain the meaning of wrinkles. We had enjoyed a wonderful weekend together, and my folks were due to leave that morning.

"Let's go!" I called.

My dad grabbed a quick cup of coffee, and we jumped into the car. The air was crisp and cool. The birds were singing and the sky was bright and clear. Committed to keeping Daniel in his current school, we faced a 30-minute drive. Daniel, a nonstop chatterbug, thoroughly enjoyed this extra time with his newfound grandpa.

We arrived to school safely and on time. While getting out of the car, my dad accidentally spilled the remains of his coffee directly into the front of his pants. He groaned and looked at me in pained despair. My dignified father looked like an incontinent, scruffy, mismatched old man. I had to bite my lip to keep from laughing.

"Oh, Daniel, look at me! I don't think I can go into your school looking like this. It looks like I wet my pants."

Daniel's eyes instantly pooled. He dropped his head, attempting to hide this rush of deep emotions. In a whispered voice he managed to say, "But Grandpa, I really wanted you to see the baby chicks."

Without hesitation, my dad scooped Daniel's hand into his and announced, "Well, what are we waiting for? Let's go to see those baby chicks."

We marched toward Daniel's school and into his first-grade classroom. Holding his jacket discreetly, my dad met his teacher, Mrs. Thompson, and some of his friends. Daniel proudly introduced him to everyone as "his grandpa." On seeing the chicks, my dad "oohed" and "aahed" over the fluffy yellow birds that danced and chirped in their cage.

The bell rang. My dad, who was kneeling by the cage, gently pulled Daniel into his arms for one last hug.

"Come back soon, okay, Grandpa?"

"You bet!"

Daniel laid his head on my dad's shoulder.

"Bye, Grandpa."

"Good-bye, Daniel."

My dad was strangely quiet as we left the school building. I thought we might share a good chuckle over the morning's events. I glanced his way. Silent tears were streaming down his face. All too aware that this little boy had known more heartache in seven short years than most people know in a lifetime, my father began to weep. Back at the car, I wrapped my arms around this scruffy old man. We hugged and allowed our tears to fall.

Ultimately it was a morning bright with sunshine and hope. Daniel had just experienced the power of a grandpa's tender love. Hurting children often need specialized help to mend the tattered places within their souls, but being loved is the first step on this journey toward healing.

I will never forget what I witnessed that spring morning between this precious child and my dad, hidden behind a face full of whiskers and a pair of coffee-stained pants.

Brenda Jank

More than half a million children are in foster care.

 ## *Learn More about Becoming a Foster Parent*

Foster parents:

- Have a deep impact on a child's life.
- Offer stability.
- Help a child to heal.
- Provide an opportunity for a child to have a second chance at childhood.
- Keep a child safe.
- Help a child reach her full potential.
- Work as members of a professional team in support of the child and his family.

Becoming a Foster Parent

While there are many variations in procedure, generally you:

- Take part in interviews to make sure foster parenting is right for you.
- Complete an application and other forms.
- Have a background check.

- Complete Foster Parenting classes.
- Take First Aid and CPR.
- See your doctor for a health exam.
- Make sure your home meets required safety standards.

Types of Homes Needed

- Traditional foster homes
- Homes for children diagnosed with specific emotional and developmental needs
- Homes for pregnant teens and/or teen mothers and their children
- Homes for groups of siblings
- Homes for gay, lesbian, bisexual, and transgender youth
- Emergency placement homes
- Respite homes

Chapter 4

TEEN TALK

Light tomorrow with today.

ELIZABETH BARRETT BROWNING

Hoop Dreams

There are victories of the soul and spirit.
Sometimes, even if you lose, you win.

ELIE WIESEL

L iving with his family in a quiet subdivision in the
town of Lacey, Washington, seventeen-year-old Alden
Tucker likes music and computers, and he's so good
at basketball that he dreams of being drafted one day by the
NBA. You might say he leads a well-rounded, fairly ordinary life, but ever since he was fifteen, Alden's life has been
anything but ordinary.

It started when he became e-mail pals with Michael
Peñon, a boy his age who had leukemia and needed a bone
marrow transplant. Alden decided to find out if he could
donate bone marrow to Michael. Since they were both of
African American, Hispanic, and Korean heritage, there was
a good chance they'd be a match.

With his parents' support, Alden set about getting tested.
Then he learned that the National Bone Marrow Donor
Program refused to test and register volunteers under the
age of eighteen who were not blood relatives of a patient in
need of a transplant. Alden feared there would be no way
to help his friend, whose condition was rapidly worsening.

"I was upset," he says. "Everybody's always talking about
how there aren't enough donors. Then when I want to help,
they say, no, you're under eighteen."

When Alden and his parents found a small blood center

that would perform the tests, the results weren't what they'd hoped for. He wasn't a match. When Michael's health took a turn for the worse, he was flown to a hospital in Cincinnati. Alden went to visit him a few weeks later, and was with Michael when he died. The death of his friend hurt him deeply, and Alden had a hard time recovering.

"Then," Alden says, "I thought maybe God was just trying to give us the big picture." Every year thousands of people die waiting for a transplant because an appropriate donor cannot be found. Perhaps a tragedy such as Michael's death could help bring about a change in age restrictions so that other lives could be saved. Alden knew that Michael would have wanted him to continue his efforts to change the rules.

Each day, about sixty-eight people receive organ transplants, while eighteen others on waiting lists die due to the lack of organs available. More than 81,000 patients await various transplants.

Normally shy and uncomfortable in the limelight, young Alden talked to lawyers, legislators, and reporters. He even went on national TV to state his case. Finally, in January 2000, his testimony before the Washington State legislature led to the enactment of sixteen words that translated Alden's struggle into law: "A person's status as a minor may not disqualify him or her from bone marrow donation."

Alden is looking forward to the day when bone marrow registries worldwide change their age restrictions. Meanwhile,

he is busy organizing Hooping for Life basketball tourna-
ments that raise money for people in need of bone marrow
transplants and signing up volunteers who want to be tested
for bone marrow donation.

And those sixteen simple words are now known as the
Michael Peñon Law.

Laurel Holliday

Get Involved in Politics

It's up to you to make your country and world a better
place. Get together with friends, family, and the community to discuss ideas and projects that can help make a difference.

Here are some tips to help get you started:

Start out small:

- Raise funds. Choose a cause close to your heart
  and create a fund-raiser. Donate the money to the
  charity or organization of your choice.
- Volunteer. Lend a hand and give your time to a
  local political organization or representatives.
- Speak out. Get your voice heard by contacting
  the press and legislators. Start a petition in your
  community; send out letters and e-mails to spread
  the word.

- Get informed. Pay attention to what others are doing so you can respond when you don't agree, or support them when you do.
- Get educated. Educate yourself so you can educate others. Ask questions. Seek answers. Know the way things are so you can influence the way they can be.

Write to your local politician:

- Be respectful. If you want the reader to be responsive to your ideas, write in a friendly and nonthreatening manner.
- Identify who you are and whom you represent. Explain why you think the issue has widespread implications for the public as a whole, not just specific interest groups.
- Keep your letter short. It should be one to two pages long when single-spaced.
- Be assertive. Focus on one issue per letter and let the reader know exactly how you feel about the issue.
- Position important points. Readers tend to skim letters; make your most important points in the first and last paragraphs.
- Establish credibility. Do your research and get your facts right.
- Establish commonality. To establish commonality, you can mention something that you both agree

on. Establish yourself as an ally working toward
the same goal.

- Request that the official take a specific action.
Ask your government representative to make a
statement in the legislature, bring your concerns
up in caucus meetings, or propose changes to legislation. Ask for a reply.

- Send a hard copy letter. It may carry more weight
than an e-mail: An original letter carries more
weight than a copied one. A letter carries more
weight than a postcard or a signature on a
petition.

- Write a bill. If you think a law is what you need to
make something happen, write one yourself.

- Lobby. Let policymakers know what you think
and how you want them to act on a specific issue.
Find out what motivates them—and motivate
them. Persuade them to change, create, or reject
legislation.

- Take part in your community by voting. Take your
kids with you when you vote. Talk about why you
think it is important to vote.

Teens have a lot of skills and talents to share, and their
families, schools, and communities will benefit by allow-
ing youth to be involved in making important decisions.

Learn how to get teens more involved. Some tips include:

- Involve your teen in making a family decision, such as:

    Purchasing a family car.
    Planning a vacation.
    Organizing a family party.
    Planning meals for the week.

- Take a teen to a political or social event in the community and help him or her learn about it and participate. Examples are election events, rallies, marches, and peaceful protests.

- Invite and expect teens to take a *real* role in these groups and activities.

- Ask for their ideas.

- Assign tasks that will require youth to do research and learn new information.

- Ask for their opinions, and then ask them to explain why they feel that way.

- Hold them accountable for their decisions and assignments.

- Show appreciation and support for their involvement.

Find out more information online at:

Teen Politics: www.teenpolitics.com
Teen Power Politics: www.teenpowerpolitics.com
Study Circles Resource Center:
    www.studycircles.org

What Kids Can Do: www.whatkidscando.org
YouthNOISE: www.youthnoise.com

 Learn More about Becoming a
Bone Marrow Donor

- Contact the National Bone Marrow Donor Program (www.marrow.org) or the National Bone Marrow Transplant Link (www.nbmtlink.org).

- Join the registry and become a potential volunteer marrow or blood stem cell donor.

- Donate your baby's umbilical cord blood at birth.

- Donate other blood products, such as whole blood or platelets (all transplant patients will need other blood products during their treatment).

- Donate your time. Contact your local donor center, recruitment groups, or cord blood bank to find out how you can get involved.

- Donate money for scientific research, donor recruitment and tissue typing, or awareness campaigns.

- Tell friends and family.

Learn More about Becoming an Organ Transplant Donor

- Contact your national organ transplant organization.

- Obtain an organ donor card at an organ bank. Fill it out, sign it, and have it signed by two witnesses.

- Remember: From just one person, six life-saving organs and nine vital tissues can be recovered and transplanted.

 ## *Donate Blood*

This is obviously a much easier and more commonplace procedure. Blood can be donated at a local hospital. Contact your local Red Cross.

Fewer than 5 percent of healthy Americans eligible to donate blood actually donate each year.

Keep On Rockin'

Love has nothing to do with what you are expecting
to get—only with what you are expecting
to give—which is everything.

KATHARINE HEPBURN

I
t's a rocking scene at the Roseland Theater in Portland,
Oregon. The band MiNDFRaME is blasting away, while
500 audience members cheer them on. Brothers
Cameron Byrd, nineteen, on lead guitar and vocals, and
Brett Byrd, seventeen, on drums, are joined by rhythm gui-
tarist John Young and bass player Jason Beito. Out front, the
brothers' father, Craig, and stepmother, Dana, watch, beaming with pride.

But there is another presence there as well, an unseen
one: the brothers' mother, Carol, who died of breast cancer
in 1999 at the age of fifty-two.

"She's always with us," Cameron and Brett say firmly. In
fact, Carol is the reason the brothers are here tonight—and
every time that MiNDFRaME plays. In her memory,
Cameron and Brett are committed to raising $1 million for
breast cancer research through their concerts and CD sales.
So far, they've reached $450,000, most of which has gone to
the Susan G. Komen Breast Cancer Foundation, chosen
because their mom had often participated in the foundation's Walk for the Cure, even before her diagnosis.

"Mom taught us to help others in any way we could. I
hope we can help find a cure for breast cancer, so other

families won't have to go through what we went through," says Brett.

> Breast cancer is the most frequently diagnosed cancer in U.S. women.

Craig knows that what makes his sons reach so high is not just how their mother died but also how she lived. "She was a teacher and a coach. The boys saw how she inspired and motivated so many people. She was an amazing woman."

In recognition of their achievement, both boys have won the Prudential Spirit of Community Awards, a national program honoring young people for outstanding acts of volunteerism.

Although neither Carol nor Craig, a financial advisor, was particularly musical, their sons showed interest at a very early age. Both played piano starting at age four. When Cameron was eleven, he found the guitar. A short while later, Brett started playing the drums. Other friends joined in, and the band was born.

All seemed rosy until Carol became ill in 1998. "In January 1999, I sat the boys down and told them that Mom was probably not going to make it and maybe we should cancel the upcoming concert that was scheduled for that March," Craig recalls.

Cameron and Brett thought about it overnight. The next morning, they went to their parents and asked if they could do the concert in their mother's honor.

Carol hugged her sons and said, "Yes, but please don't do it for me forever. Play because you love your music. The best way to honor me is to follow your hearts and talents." She died one month later.

The original intent was to do just one fund-raising concert, but when people found out why the boys were performing, the support was so strong that the brothers decided to keep going. MiNDFRaME has played more than fifty concerts, sung the national anthem at an Oakland A's major league baseball game, performed on NBC-TV's *Today* show and *The Rosie O'Donnell Show,* and were Grand Marshals for the Rose Festival in Portland.

The boys write all their own music. Cameron has written one song about his mother, "I'm Okay," which he plays at every concert. When he sings, "Our hearts are always with you now/I'm sure you're with us too," it's tough not to wonder what Carol would think if she could see her boys today.

Cameron knows: "She'd say, 'Keep on rockin'!'"

And they do. For her.

Beth Levine

Ten Ways Teens Can Help Others through Volunteering

1. Younger children

Be a tutor or assist in after-school programs. Volunteer in a day care center, assisting the teachers by preparing snacks, playing with the children, and helping with games and activities. During the summer, you can serve as a counselor in a local summer day camp or recreation center.

2. Seniors

Nursing homes, retirement communities, and adult day care programs need volunteers. Share a special talent, help with arts or other activities, or serve as a friendly visitor for some of the residents who have very few visitors. Read mail to residents, help write letters, go for walks, play games, create cooking and art projects, or simply talk and exchange stories. You can also help older adults remain in their homes by performing yard work and other tasks.

3. Hospitals

Volunteer in a local hospital. Help deliver flowers, books, and mail. Read to the patients. Stock nursing and medical supplies. Put on a play for the children. Assist with office tasks.

4. Computers

Many organizations need the assistance of technologically

savvy young volunteers. Many need assistance with Web site development, spreadsheet and database development and maintenance, data entry, and other computer tasks. Other agencies need volunteers to serve as computer tutors for children and/or older adults.

5. Hunger and homelessness

Serve food to the hungry in a local shelter, help build houses for people who are homeless, work in a housing facility or shelter for the homeless, or provide office assistance to an organization whose goal is to combat poverty.

6. Arts organizations

Teens interested in the arts may offer their time to theater groups, visual arts organizations, or writing and photography projects. Summer volunteers may serve as counselors in a summer arts camp.

7. Environmental and conservation groups

Work outdoors doing cleanup projects or help your local park department with landscape maintenance and trail development. Lead hiking groups or tree-planting initiatives. Assist environmental education agencies with everything from research and development to advocacy and office tasks.

8. Docents and tour guides

Be a docent or tour guide at a museum, aquarium, historic site, or botanical garden. These venues need help setting up and maintaining exhibits, directing guests, and conducting special events.

9. Television and video production

Help out at your local cable access station. Many run programs that teach participants how to use the video equipment. To find out about the cable access opportunities in your area, contact your local cable access station.

10. Animals

More comfortable around animals than people? Local animal shelters and veterinary offices often need assistance from caring teens. Or help out at a nearby horse stable. Clean the facilities, answer phones, tend to the animals. Look in the Yellow Pages, under "Veterinary" or "Animal Shelters." Ask to speak to the office manager or veterinarian.

 Remember

- Teen volunteerism has reached its highest level in fifty years.
- Seventy-three percent of America's 60 million young people believe they can make a difference in their communities.
- Teenagers volunteer 2.4 billion hours annually.

Here's to You, Mrs. Robinson

There are two ways of spreading light:
to be the candle or the mirror that reflects it.

Edith Wharton

I was fifteen, and my mother suggested that I think about going to boarding school. Mom was searching for a new husband, and I wasn't cooperating. One, I loved my dad. Two, going out with Mom and her dates was one of my worst nightmares. Just one, mind you.

She felt so guilty about leaving me home alone that she kept inviting, then nagging, me to join in all the fun.

Then one day she asked me if I'd like to go away to school. "I heard of a boarding school, the Scarborough School. It's near home. It's supposed to be very progressive. You'd come home weekends. Perhaps you'd be happier."

I worried about missing my friends and not fitting in, but decided that it wasn't a bad idea. The morning I arrived I was assigned to share a room with four other girls. I'd expected to have my own room. I just sat on my bed and listened to them gab. They were old timers.

The first night in boarding school was one of the loneliest in my life. That evening, we all walked to the school cafeteria for dinner. Students were given assigned seats, and one of the teaching staff was at each table.

When I came back with my tray, I sat down next to Mrs. Edith Robinson. I remember her curly gray hair, her plaid skirt, her hazel eyes that seemed inquisitive in a nice way. I played with my food.

"Where is your home?" Mrs. Robinson asked.

"Manhattan," I said. I could hardly get the word out.

"Oh, that's fortunate. You'll be able to go home weekends."

I nodded. My dessert was in front of me, but I couldn't eat it. I was convinced that I'd made the wrong decision. Tears dripped down my face. The more I tried to wipe them away, the faster they flowed.

"I teach third grade," Mrs. Robinson said as she handed me a tissue. "There's a little girl in my class who's always had a hard time reading. I wonder if you'd consider tutoring Elizabeth. I think she's scared of grownups. Do you have free time, say at three o'clock, to come to my room and help her?"

"I can try." Three o'clock! That was the hour I dreaded. Classes would be over. Who would I talk to? What else did I have to do?

The next day and every afternoon after that, I rushed to Mrs. Robinson's third-grade room. There, Elizabeth and I sat on a blue couch in the back of the room while Mrs. Robinson worked at her desk and occasionally chatted with us. Often I stayed even later, chatting with Mrs. Robinson, confiding my thoughts and worries as I erased the board and straightened the desks.

Within a month, Elizabeth had started to read and I had my own private room. That gave me new confidence. One afternoon, I realized I'd made three new girlfriends and was no longer a loner.

Mentoring has been shown to boost self-confidence in youth by 81 percent.

Right before summer vacation, my mother called with a big surprise. She was going to sign me up for Elizabeth Arden's Charm School. They'd teach me about things like good grooming and posture, and I'd make lots of friends.

"I have lots of friends," I argued. "And I don't want to be charming."

"That's just the reason you need to go." My mother was angry; I hadn't appreciated her great idea.

"I won't go and you can't make me!"

In the days that followed, my mother backed off and let me stay. It wasn't until years later that I learned that Mrs. Robinson had written to my mother and explained that I had changed. I was a beautiful girl now, she said, and had good friends. Perhaps my mother hadn't realized how much I'd matured during my sophomore year at Scarborough.

My mother complained to the principal, but he managed to calm her down. I never knew what words passed between him and Mrs. Robinson, but I realized that my mentor had put her job on the line.

After I graduated from Scarborough School, I attended the University of Colorado, and Mrs. Robinson and I corresponded for many years. After college, I got my degree in special education, working with emotionally disturbed children.

I lost track of Mrs. Robinson after I married and had children of my own. My attempts to find her were futile. The school had changed hands many times and had no records of her whereabouts. But she still resides somewhere within me.

Often, when I see a child who looks like she can't seem to find the words, or who dreads the recess bell, I remember Mrs. Robinson's heartfelt offer to tutor her student. And I remember Elizabeth, who helped me through that difficult year—by needing me.

Joan Halperin

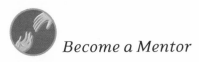 ## Become a Mentor

What Is a Mentor?

A mentor is an experienced person who goes out of his or her way to help a mentee set important life goals and develop the skills to reach them.

- An *informal* mentor provides coaching, listening, advice, sounding board reactions, or other help in an unstructured, casual manner.

- A *formal* or *enhanced informal* mentor agrees to an ongoing, planned partnership that focuses on helping the mentee reach specific goals over a designated period.

What Is Mentoring?

Mentoring is the presence of one or many caring individuals who, along with parents and guardians, provide youth with support, counsel, friendship, reinforcement, and constructive example. It is a proven strategy for placing adults into the lives of children and youth.

Every mentoring relationship is shaped by the different personalities, interests, and needs of each mentor and child. The activities they choose, whether they just talk, play sports, or read together, will reflect these unique qualities. But the real force for positive change comes from the fruits of the relationship itself. Trust. Confidence. Enthusiasm. Growth. And most important, fun.

Who Is Qualified to Be a Mentor?

People just like you.

A mentor is someone who cares, listens, and offers encouragement. Mentors are partners in change. They help children develop their strengths and talents by supporting the efforts of other significant people such as parents and teachers.

Mentors are:	Mentors are not:
Good listeners	Baby-sitters
Caring friends	Surrogate parents
Confidence builders	Therapists
Ordinary people	Saviors

According to a research study, young people who meet regularly with mentors are:

- 46 percent less likely to begin using illegal drugs.
- 27 percent less likely to begin drinking alcohol.
- 52 percent less likely to skip school.
- 33 percent less likely to hit someone.

Children are not the only ones whose lives can be changed by mentoring. Mentoring benefits all of society: Healthy, educated, and nurtured children grow up to be productive adults and responsible parents. They may even grow up to be mentors themselves someday.

Many teens also mentor younger children.

For more information on becoming a mentor:

- Go to www.savethechildren.org/mentors.
- Call toll-free 1-877-BE-A-MENTOR or check out www.mentoring.org.
- Contact Big Brothers Big Sisters of America at www.bbbsa.org.
- Visit the Partners Mentoring Association at www.partnersmentoring.org.

Steering the Course

Help thy brother's boat across, and lo!
Thine own has reached the shore.

HINDU PROVERB

While working with an outdoor education program one summer, I had the opportunity to meet many teenagers. One I will never forget. Mike seemed anxious as he approached the kids huddled in clusters. A skinny guy, taller than the others, his brown hair shielded eyes that seemed to be forever studying the ground. He was one of the last to arrive for the weeklong camp that brought together high school children from diverse backgrounds, and as cliques were fast to form, Mike found himself a step behind.

There are nearly 10,000 camps in the United States, with more than 6 million children attending camp each summer.

During the seven days, the teens engaged in the challenges of rock climbing and a high-ropes course. Throughout the experience, the group continued to develop its identity, and an unspoken pecking order emerged. Many of the participants were agile and quick learners, but Mike was at that awkward age when his limbs didn't quite fit his torso and he struggled with some of the more taxing aspects of the program. Yet, despite his own difficulties, Mike consistently offered suggestions and would help anyone who was having trouble. Sometimes that help came simply in the form of his warm smile.

As time passed, all the campers were looking forward to the week's culminating event: an overnight canoe trip down the river.

On the morning of the trip, showers were forecast, and most of the group was decked out in the latest well-fitting outdoor gear. Mike emerged from his cabin completely shrouded by an enormous yellow parka. This was the type of garment commonly seen covering diehard baseball fans who were waiting out a rain delay, and it was clear that it caused Mike a bit of embarrassment.

They headed out, and the rains eventually let up, but strong breezes continued to challenge the new paddlers trying to find a straight course down the river. As was common practice, we traded boat partners periodically, and Mike always found himself in a staff canoe.

For safety, the staff boats travel in point and sweep positions—the first and last boats in our group, respectively. While each boat is responsible for keeping an eye on the boats in front of and behind them at all times, the line can get strung out over a good distance. Mike and I were in the sweep boat when an opportunity presented itself. A long flat stretch of river lay ahead, so I called out for the point boat to trade positions. Since this normally meant that everyone had to stop during the changeover, Mike didn't like my suggestion; it was late in the day, and the group was looking forward to reaching the end.

Nevertheless, I handed Mike our spare paddle and asked him to grab his poncho, stretch it between the two paddles, and hoist it up into the air. As the tailwind filled our new sail, we effortlessly cruised past the other boats and through the remaining section of river. From my vantage point, it was hard to tell if it was Mike's sail or his chest that was sticking out further.

That night around the campfire, Mike was clearly up to his speed with his peers and the center of attention, with the rest of the kids asking him to retell the excitement of our victorious river run.

Years later, I ran into Mike working at a local ice cream shop. At first, I didn't recognize him. Here was a confident, broad-shouldered guy looking me in the eye. He wore his uniform with pride. Our exchange was brief and pleasant as he promptly filled our order. He was leaving for college soon, he told us, and was hoping to take a weekend trip with his friends.

When he asked for directions to the river we had paddled, I smiled and drew a map.

Ryan Furer

Learn More about Self-Esteem and How It Affects Teens

Teens with high self-esteem tend to be more content. They bounce back faster from a crisis. They are not afraid to take risks. They do not waste time worrying about problems. They believe in taking action to solve any problems that may crop up. They tend to be more flexible and adjust easily to changing situations. They are not commitment-shy when it comes to relationships, because they are not uptight about compromising and giving of themselves.

It's clear that a child who has self-esteem is happier, more creative, better adjusted, more confident, and resilient.

Low self-esteem can affect just about every aspect of a teen's life. If teenagers feel bad or unsure about themselves, they may be unable to participate fully in any activity for fear of failure. It is important to remember that being a teenager means making mistakes, and this is a painful but necessary way to learn. Teens can't handle everything perfectly all the time and shouldn't expect to. They don't have to try to face up to what everyone else thinks they should be, but should make sure that they are proud of their decisions and actions.

Teens should not base their opinion of themselves on what others say or measure themselves against others' accomplishments. Teens are individuals and should be encouraged to develop a strong self-image.

Here are some tips for increasing a teen's self-esteem:

- When you feel good about them, mention it to them.
- Be generous with praise.
- Teach teens to practice making positive self-statements.
- Avoid criticism that takes the form of ridicule or shame.
- Teach teens about decision making and how to recognize when they have made a good decision.
- Encourage teens to ask for what they want assertively, pointing out that there is no guarantee that they will get it. Reinforce them for asking.
- Encourage teens to develop hobbies and interests that give them pleasure and that they can pursue independently.
- Help teens learn to focus on their strengths by pointing out to them all the things they can do.
- Laugh with teens and encourage them to laugh at themselves. A good sense of humor and the ability to make light of life are important ingredients for increasing one's overall enjoyment.

A Lesson Learned

If the world is to be healed through human efforts,
I am convinced it will be by ordinary people,
people whose love for this life is even
greater than their fear.

JOANNA MACY

A s an eighth-grade teacher, I was shocked when I entered my classroom. I had stumbled upon the climax of a vicious fight.

Martha pulled out of the clinch and clawed at Lydia's face and arms, and Lydia fought back just as vehemently. Quickly, I pulled the two girls apart. Lydia returned to the crowd of students who had been cheering her on, while Martha slumped into my arms, by turns weeping, clinging, and beating at my chest. This lasted no more than two minutes, before Martha pulled away and ran off—to the office, I hoped.

"Could someone please tell me what just happened here?" I asked, still shaking. By now the class was moving to their seats, a charged silence gripping the room. Lydia was tending her wounds and was near tears herself. What had aroused such anger in an ordinarily calm group? They began the story:

"Go back to Mexico," taunted the note to Raul.

"Go back to Africa," said the message Derrick had received.

"You belong in China," Mai read on her scrap of paper.

It seemed that during the last period Martha had deliberately gone around the room delivering a written or spoken slur to each student about his or her heritage.

The principal's shadow preceded her entrance into the classroom. "I want to know all the details of what happened here," she opened, "and I expect you to see that the whole class is suitably punished, since, as I understand it, they all played a part in egging on the fight. This behavior, especially from eighth graders, will not be tolerated. Martha will be suspended until Monday, and I'll call later for Lydia. I want you to teach these students a lesson." Palpable silence and thirty pairs of eyes followed me from the door to the desk.

The kids told me that Martha had been steadily burning all her bridges: putting other students down, isolating herself at lunch, and lashing out at former friends. Why would a bright girl be so self-destructive? As we pieced recent events together, we began to understand that Martha was literally begging for attention and had found a foolproof way to get it. Now the kids themselves asked the key question: "Why did Martha want us to hate her?" A shaking, somber Lydia raised her hand.

"Look, you guys will think I'm really weird, but I feel sorry for her. We were good friends until the third grade and then she did something kind of like today. I remember I used to see marks on her arms and legs that didn't come from running into walls like she said. Remember the black eye she got? I think I know why she's acting this way. I did the same thing in fifth grade."

We all held our breath, astonished at Lydia's courage. "I

think Martha hates herself because she's getting beaten up at home. When my dad used to beat me and my mom, he made us feel like we were dirt and deserved it. When he beat my brother, Tony would turn around and hit me so hard you can't believe it, and it wasn't because Tony was mad at me. I understand the pain Martha is going through because I've been there."

Close to 900,000 children per year are victims of maltreatment, whether they suffer from neglect or physical, sexual, or psychological abuse.

Lydia's gentle but passionate voice trailed off. Her classmates were somber. And now the principal wanted me to punish them? We felt that we understood more about what had probably triggered Martha's comments, and the conversation turned to how she might feel when she returned to school on Monday after her suspension.

"You feel like everyone's staring at you and won't accept you back. It's pretty scary," said Derrick, a frequent suspendee.

"What about a party?" I suggested tentatively, really just thinking out loud.

Within seconds, they were wondrous steps ahead of me in making healing happen. "We could each bring something like cookies or punch!" "Don't forget napkins and cups!" "I can bring a cooler with ice!" "How about a banner that says, 'Welcome Back and We Love You Martha'?" Every talent and appetite in the class were soon represented, and it was Lydia herself who circulated the sign-up sheet, which quickly overflowed.

My follow-up conversation with the principal was brief. "You've taken care of the class, I trust?" she asked me.

"Yes, we came up with a consequence that put every-body to work," I responded.

Monday morning, Martha entered the festively deco-rated classroom surprised, then bashful, when she saw the banner, and finally showed a tentative smile of appreciation. Lydia was the first in a long line of kids to hug her. After more hugs and through her tears, Martha apologized for the insulting notes and comments.

"That was an ugly thing to do, as ugly as I sometimes feel on the inside." She looked around the room at the faces of her classmates before continuing. "I'm not really ready to talk about it, but I know you guys will be there when I am."

Indeed, the students had learned a lesson. And so had I.

Karen E. Eifler

Help Prevent Child Abuse and Neglect

Reach out. Anything you do to support kids and parents can help reduce the stress that often leads to abuse and neglect.

- Support a parent you know. Ask how their children are doing. Draw on your own experiences to provide reassurance. If a parent seems to be struggling, offer to baby-sit or run errands, or just lend a friendly ear. Show you understand.

- Talk to your neighbors about looking out for one another's children. Encourage a supportive spirit among parents in your apartment building or on your block. Show that you are involved.

- Give your used clothing, furniture, and toys for use by another family. This can help relieve the stress of financial burdens that parents sometimes take out on their kids.

- Volunteer your time and money for programs in your community that support children and families, like parent support groups or day care centers.

Raise the issue. By educating yourself and others, you can help your community prevent child abuse and neglect from happening in the first place.

- Check out child abuse prevention publications (and other resources) and photocopy information to post in your workplace, apartment building, library, laundromat, church, beauty parlor, supermarket, or school.

- Contact your school district, library, or faith group about support programs for parents and how you can help. If no programs exist, encourage the group to sponsor classes and develop resources for parents.

- Wear a blue ribbon and tell people that it stands for the prevention of child abuse and neglect.

- Call or write your elected officials and ask them to support funding for parent support and child abuse prevention programs. Enclose copies of articles on child abuse and neglect from your local newspaper.

- Write to the editor of your local newspaper sharing what you've learned about child abuse and neglect. Point out that preventing child abuse and neglect is an important investment in the future of your community.

Remember the risk factors. Child abuse and neglect occur in all segments of our society, but the risk factors are greater in families where parents:

- Seem to be having economic, housing, or personal problems.

- Are isolated from their family or community.

- Have difficulty controlling anger or stress.

- Are dealing with physical or mental health issues.

- Abuse alcohol or drugs.

- Appear uninterested in the care, nourishment, or safety of their children.

By helping parents who might be struggling with any of these challenges, you reduce the likelihood that their children will be abused or neglected. Reach out to the children, too, and show them that you care.

Recognize the warning signs. The behavior of children may signal abuse or neglect long before any change in physical appearance. Some of the signs may include:

- Nervousness around adults
- Aggression toward adults or other children
- Inability to stay awake or to concentrate for extended periods
- Sudden, dramatic changes in personality or activities
- Unnatural interest in sex
- Frequent or unexplained bruises or injuries
- Low self-esteem
- Poor hygiene

If you see these signs in any children you know, reach out to them and to their parents and offer a helping hand.

Report suspected abuse or neglect. If you suspect abuse or neglect may be occurring, report it. To find out how, call information or contact your department of social services listed under "Government Agencies" in the phone book. If you think a child is in immediate danger, call the police.

For more information on how you can prevent child abuse and neglect, please visit www.preventchildabuse.org

Chapter 5

FOR THE HOLIDAYS

*Blessed is the season which engages
the whole world in a conspiracy of love.*

HAMILTON WRIGHT MABIE

Christmas Angels

If I can ease one life the aching,
Or cool one pain,
Or help one fainting robin
Unto his nest again,
I shall not live in vain.

EMILY DICKINSON

I t was December 23. My two young children and I lived in a tiny, cramped house. Between going to college and supporting my kids completely on my own, I knew that Christmas was looking bleak.

It was late, almost eleven. The snow was falling softly, silently. I was wrapped in a blanket, sitting at the window watching the powdery flakes flutter in the moonlight, when my front door vibrated from the knocking of a pounding fist.

Alarmed, I wondered who would be at my home so late on a snowy winter night. I peeked through the curtain on my front door to find several strangers grinning from ear to ear, their arms laden with boxes and bags.

Confused, I opened the door.

"Are you Susan?" The man stepped forward and pushed a box at me.

Nodding, unable to find my voice, I was sure they thought I was mentally deficient.

"These are for you." The woman thrust another box at me with a huge, beaming smile. The porch light and the snow falling behind her cast a glow on her dark hair, lending her an angelic appearance.

I looked down into the box. It was filled with treats, a fat turkey, and all the makings of a traditional Christmas dinner. My eyes filled with tears as the realization of what they were doing washed over me.

Finally coming to my senses, I invited them in. The man and woman entered, followed by two children staggering under the weight of wrapped boxes. This wonderful family, total strangers to me, somehow knew exactly what we needed. They brought gifts for each of us and a full buffet for me to cook on Christmas Day. Visions of a beautiful, "normal" holiday danced in my head. The desperate prayers of a single mom were heard.

Then they handed me an envelope, offered another round of grins, and hugged me. Wishing me a Merry Christmas, they disappeared into the night as suddenly as they had appeared.

I wrapped myself in my blanket, sat at the window, and opened the envelope. A shower of bills flitted to the floor. Gathering them up, I began to count the bills. One hundred dollars.

Even though my mysterious angels had showered me with gifts, they had somehow understood how desperately I needed the money. There was no way they could have known it, but I had just received a notice from the gas company telling me that they were going to cut me off for nonpayment of my bill. I simply didn't have the money and feared my little family would be without heat by Christmas. The envelope of cash would give us warmth and a tree for

Christmas. Suddenly, we had all we needed and more.

I looked at my children sleeping soundly, and through my tears I smiled the first happy, free-of-worry smile in a long, long time. My smile turned into a grin as I thought about the next day, Christmas Eve. One visit from complete strangers had magically turned a painful day into a special one we would always remember.

Several years have passed and I have since remarried. We are happy and richly blessed. Every year since that Christmas of 1993, we choose a family less blessed than we are. We bring them carefully selected gifts, food and treats, and as much money as we can spare. It's our way of passing on what was given to us and hoping that the cycle continues.

Susan Farr Fahncke

Consumers plan to spend an average of $518.44 on gifts this year, $34.18 on decorations, $25.79 on greeting cards and postage, $79.42 on candy and food, and $14.06 on flowers.

Be a Holiday Angel

These simple gift-giving tips can help you put a smile on someone else's face:

- Be a friend. Spend time helping people around the house, baby-sitting their children, or taking them out. Observe their interests, needs, and desires.

- Gift baskets are easy and abundant. Most gift basket companies make themed baskets, which are presentable and personal. A basket can be delivered to the home of the stranger. Search your local directory for gift basket providers near you or visit gift basket Web sites on the Internet.

- Great Gifts is a wonderful nonprofit organization that gives simple gifts to people all over the world: items like hens for a school of orphans in Jerusalem and a self-powered lifeline radio to a family in Zambia, where 1 in 5 adults is living with HIV/AIDS. (www.great-gifts.org)

- Flowers can brighten a person's day. Include seed packets, so the recipient can plant their own garden.

- Anonymous gifts, especially sums of money, can raise suspicion. If you offer a donation, include a heartfelt card that explains who you are and features a sincere salutation.

- Prepare a basket of recipes and ingredients for simple meals. Offer to teach the recipient to cook the meals. Make a personalized cookbook.

- Assemble a school kit. Include pencils, notebooks, tools, and favorite books. You can also offer to tutor.

- Write a poem or story to wish someone well.

- Offer to clean and fix someone's home. Collect household items, furnishings, and kitchenware from neighbors.

- Create a vacation package. Include maps, advice, and guidebooks. Lend travel equipment, such as tents, sleeping bags, and luggage. Everyone needs time away.

Mr. Holland's Thanksgiving Dinner

*Giving connects two people, the giver and
the receiver, and this connection gives
birth to a new sense of belonging.*

DEEPAK CHOPRA

In 1976, still a newlywed couple, my husband, Gary, and
I lived in a small Georgia town. We were doing pretty
well; we were in good health, had few bills, and made
a comfortable middle-class living. We rented a modest two-
bedroom apartment on the ground floor of a small building. Above us lived a feeble elderly man named Mr. Holland.

We were young, free spirited, and busy. Mr. Holland, on
the other hand, seemed like such a crabby fellow. He never
smiled. He complained about our music and our laughter
and constantly peeked at us through the window when we
barbecued in the patio area behind our dwelling. In fact,
we weren't inconsiderate neighbors; my husband was a firefighter and auxiliary police officer, and we made every effort
to be mindful of others. During the two years that we lived
there, Mr. Holland rarely left the apartment, and we only
saw him have visitors on two occasions.

I loved to cook, and being a newlywed wife I really got
into it. I decided that instead of going to Mom and Dad's
place for Thanksgiving, I really wanted to cook for my husband at home. I started the day before, and by midday on
Thanksgiving, everything was perfect. I had prepared a wonderfully sumptuous feast.

Even though it was broad daylight, we lit a candle to add a little romance. Gary said a Thanksgiving prayer and, just as we looked at each other and smiled, we heard a kitchen chair scrub across the floor directly above, and our smiles faded. Mr. Holland.

"I wonder what he's having for dinner?" I asked Gary.

But we both knew the answer.

So I got up from the table, found my large china platter, and loaded it up—the works, turkey dressing, all the veggies, homemade bread. I took another plate and spooned in some pie and peach cobbler for dessert.

> In 2002, about 271 million turkeys were raised. It is estimated that 46 million of those turkeys were eaten at Thanksgiving, 22 million at Christmas, and 19 million at Easter.

My husband and I carried the dishes up the stairs and gently knocked on Mr. Holland's door. He answered. His short, wiry frame and slouched shoulders made him look like life had beaten him down, which it probably had.

"We figured you didn't want to do a bunch of cooking, so we brought you some dinner."

Joy erupted on his face. His whole personality seemed to change. Suddenly he seemed more open, as if he had been waiting a very long time for someone, anyone, to make that kind of gesture. Through his misty eyes, he offered a few thankful words, and we barely made it down the stairs and into our apartment before our own tears flowed. We silently held each other for a while before returning to our dinner and, later that evening, visiting with family and friends.

The next day, the doorbell rang, and there stood Mr. Holland with a radiant smile. He had my dishes in one hand and a jar of hard candy in the other.

"For you," he said with a glow in his eye.

"Please come in," I said.

"No, I can't right now, but I did want to tell you how much it meant that you thought of me last night. I get lonely a lot, especially around the holidays. It really was the nicest holiday I've had in a long, long time."

When he walked up the stairs that day, his step seemed a little lighter. After that, he always had a smile for us, and we waved and chatted when we saw each other. I know that he was very grateful for our small gesture, but I felt that we were the lucky ones. We got to see that beautiful smile and peek into that sweet heart, and experience what Thanksgiving truly can be.

Amelia Ashford-Phillips

Be Thankful and Give Some of Your Time

- Volunteer at a soup kitchen, serving Thanksgiving dinners to homeless people. Soup kitchens provide one of the basics of life—nourishing meals—for the homeless and other disadvantaged members of the community. Volunteers generally do much of the work, including picking up donations of food, preparing meals, serving them, and cleaning up afterward. To volunteer your services, contact your local soup kitchen, mobile food program, shelter, or religious center.

- Start a canned food or clothing drive in your neighborhood or community.

- Participate in a local chapter event with:

  Meals on Wheels: www.mowa.org
  Red Cross: www.redcross.org
  United Way: www.unitedway.org

- Take part in a local charity walk or run that day.

- Bring handmade Thanksgiving cards and baked goods to a nearby convalescent home, shelter, or orphanage.

A Pillowcase Full

*The luxury of doing good surpasses
every other personal enjoyment.*

JOHN GAY

When I was t eight years old, my thoughts were, like most third graders', on Halloween. Although I was trying to concentrate on cursive writing and the 4s times tables at school, my mind was still at home. Home was where my costume could be found.

It was beautiful. I was going to be an angel with wings. Even though my mother had made them out of cardboard and leftover Christmas tinsel, I thought that she had made magic. It was certainly an improvement over last year's costume, when I had been a female Frankenstein. That costume had been a hand-me-down from my brother Kevin.

Just fourteen months separated us, and we had to share everything—including germs. The morning of Halloween, I was surprised to find out that I could hardly swallow. As my brother hung his head down from the top bunk, he did not have to say a word. I knew that he was sick, too. *Mumps!* Nothing could have been more terrible, especially on Halloween.

As the rain fell that night, anytime I looked at my beautiful costume, my tears followed. My mother tried to make the best out of it, telling us how much fun it would be to give out candy. She kept reciting the old homily, "'Tis Blessed to Give as Well as Receive." I admit it was exciting to see what television character or creature our neighborhood friends would be, but it still was not quite as thrilling as going trick-or-treating.

After placing bubble gum and Dum Dum suckers in a witch's pumpkin, Mom told us that it was time for bed. As Kevin climbed to the top bunk and I crawled into the bottom, we heard a knock.

"Kids, come to the front door!" my mother called.

There, framed in the front porch light, we saw the four Montgomery children. They handed a pillowcase full of candy to my brother and one to me. We were in shock.

"Please thank your mother for this very thoughtful idea," said my mother.

"But Mom didn't tell us to do this," explained Bonnie, the oldest child. "We just thought it was the right thing to do."

> During Halloween, consumers will buy 20 million pounds of candy corn. Each American will consume 25.2 pounds of candy and will spend on average $55 for this sweet satisfaction.

As the Montgomery children walked away, I noticed that they only had two pillowcases between the four of them. They had actually given away their *own* pillowcases—full of candy. I couldn't believe that anybody would do this, especially when their mother hadn't *made* them do it.

Mom let us stay up and sort our treats. As we put the Pixie straws, Tootsie rolls, and black-and-orange peanut butter kisses into piles, I was surprised to find a number of miniature chocolate bars. The Montgomery children hadn't even picked out the really good stuff!

Stephanie Ray Brown

 ## *Trick-or-Treat for UNICEF*

What does Halloween mean in your family? Obviously, children love the spookiness of the night and the thrill of coming home with bags of colorful candy loot. For many, it also means little orange boxes rattling with coins that provide precious help to children all over the world.

- Get your "Trick-or-Treat for UNICEF" box and think of those in need.

  The tradition began in Philadelphia in 1950 when a youth group collected $17 in decorated milk cartons on Halloween to help children overseas. Since then, trick-or-treaters have collected more than $105 million. Today, UNICEF works in more than 160 countries and territories, providing children with life-saving medicine, proper nutrition, clean water, education, and emergency relief. Their current goal is to vaccinate 70 million children against poliomyelitis over the course of ten days, as part of an initiative to put an end to this paralyzing disease.

Although children will be hitting the haunted streets in anticipation of what they will get, they are also naturally empathetic and eager to give. When kids have concrete examples of how their donations will be used, they're even more excited to help.

- Remember, those pennies add up!

Seventy cents buys twelve pencils for a classroom.

Six cents buys three vitamin A tablets to protect a child against blindness.

One dollar buys 20 tablets that will purify 4.4 gallons of water.

Four dollars buys a rake for use in a school vegetable garden.

- Go to www.unicef.org and download a volunteer badge and your own official UNICEF box to fold and glue.

- While you're sharing ideas for the best costume ever and telling ghastly tales of terror, use this time to remind kids that, while getting is awesome, giving is even better!

Create a Neighborly Needs Day

If your family would rather spend some time getting to know your neighbors, a great alternative tradition to trick-or-treating is a "Neighborly Needs Day."

- In late October, choose a seasonal chore that would be helpful to perform as a courtesy for your neighbors. For instance, your family might consider cleaning windows, raking leaves, or washing cars together.

- Then preselect a manageable area of your neighborhood and previsit each of the neighbors you would like to volunteer for. It is best if you visit as a family so that it's obvious that parents will be involved in the project.

- Explain to your neighbors that rather than trick-or-treating this year, your family would like to serve each neighbor by helping with a chore. Ask them if it would be all right to come by on a specific day to complete your task. Assure them that you will bring all the necessary supplies: rakes, garbage bags, cleaning supplies.

- Be aware that your neighbors will be astounded at first, but that your family's servant spirit will form an unforgettable bond with them for years to come. After a day of helping your neighbors, take your family out for ice cream or pizza and talk about how it feels to give to other people.

Think of Other Creative Ways to Do Some Halloween Good

- Carve pumpkins and leave them on the pumpkin-less porches of your neighbors.

- Host or coordinate a Charity Costume Ball or Masquerade for adults, or Haunted House for children, and donate the proceeds to an activity for a children's home.

- Create a program so children in unsafe neighborhoods can visit a local university and trick-or-treat throughout the dorms.

Picking Up Jesus

How far that little candle throws his beams!
So shines a good deed in a weary world.

WILLIAM SHAKESPEARE

I
t was Christmas Eve 1991, and I was driving the streets of San Francisco for Yellow Cab. The cool dark night found me restless, driving people here and there. Most were happy, in search of friends and relatives.

I drove folks to and from parties in Nob Hill, carried people warm and glowing from Union Street drinks, and others sated with food from the Avenues. Picked up a middle-aged couple in Park Merced, then a bunch of doctors at UC. Back down Geary to downtown, then turned toward North Beach. The bars were crowded, and I made good money that night, more than $200 with a lot of fares and generous tips. Unlike me, my passengers generally knew where they wanted to be that evening.

Christmas has always been a mixture of complex emotions for me. Growing up Jewish puts Christmas at odds with my upbringing and heritage, and it's difficult to ignore the pervasive holiday spirit, gift giving, commercial appeals, and Christian as well as secular frivolity that leads up to December 25. I'm always left outside looking in—to somebody else's party. The lights just aren't as bright as I sigh and make my way in the world. I try to force joy and happiness into my heart, but usually end up sad and distracted. Driving a cab is as good a way as any to beat the holiday blues.

I was antsy, wistful, and envious driving that December 24. And hungry too, since almost every late-night restaurant in the city was closed for the holiday. I did, however, find one burrito place open on Mission and 30th, packed with revelers and loners. All kinds of people were there, so I knew I wasn't the only one. I bought a smoky Christmas Eve burrito and ate it back in the cab, listening to the news on the radio. Not much happening in the world, it seemed.

I had just finished my dinner and was about to hit the streets when an old Chevy Nova came up silently behind my cab. It parked close, too close for my comfort, and blocked my exit. This is a danger signal to all cabbies; you always need an exit. A guy climbed out and approached my cab as I tensed and waited for any sign of trouble.

He raised his hands to surrender. "Yo, man, can you help me?" he asked. "I'm lost. Can you help me find Arago Street?" He slurred a little, and his voice was thick.

I looked him over. He was shorter than me but built up, like a weightlifter or an ex-con. He had a heavy Hispanic accent that I couldn't place. He could break me into little pieces if he wanted. He was drunk. This was certain.

I got out of the cab, still wary but relaxing a bit. He didn't seem violent. "What do you need?" I asked.

He said, "Hmm, can you help me find Arago Street? I have friends. . . . They are expecting me." He rolled his *r*'s on *Arago*. He played with the top button on his jacket.

I was feeling more at ease and asked, "What's your name?"

"No names, friend, no names." He smiled as he said this.

I repeated the question and wondered about this man.

He replied, "I might be Jesus." And gave me a goofy grin.

I raised my eyebrows at this statement. I might have coughed.

"Don't worry, man, I'm not crazy." He paused, then said, "I was in Airborne. Army Airborne. Let me show you." And at that he took off his bomber jacket, then his shirt to show me a huge Double A tattoo on his biceps, indicating Army Airborne.

The conversation seemed weird. A military guy? What did it mean? I knew that I didn't want to see any more of his body. I stammered, "Yeah, well, ugh, put your clothes on. What do you want?"

"Arago Street. That's all. I'm lost." He opened his arms as he said this.

I sighed, then pulled out my creased AAA city map. We studied the map on the hood of the cab. Actually I studied it. He repeated the name of the obscure street, and I finally found it deep in the Outer Mission, near City College. I explained where it was, but he didn't comprehend. I looked him in the eye and said, "I'll drive you."

"No, no. I drive." He was pointing at himself.

I laughed and shook my head. He was in no condition to drive to his friends' house or anywhere else. "I don't think that's a good idea," I said, though I realized he was serious.

He protested. "No, I'm okay. I drive. I follow you, you show me the way. I follow *you!*" He smiled and gestured for me to get in the car.

This could get dangerous; he was drunk and disoriented. Besides, it had money loser written all over it. However, I figured it would be good to somehow safely get him off the road. I knew he was going on with or without me. I made the decision.

"All right, all right. I'm turning the meter on, and you follow me, close, but don't hit me! And be careful." I raised my voice. "Got it?" This could be chancy.

"Okay, yes friend, yes, thank you. I follow you." He nodded in approval.

We got into our cars. He revved his engine way up, and I took a deep breath and hoped that this wouldn't be a disaster. He backed up with a jerk and let me pass. I slowly took some back streets on toward Alemany. He followed wildly, far away, then coming up very close to my bumper. I tried to keep a safe distance between us as I checked the map. I made a few careful turns as we snaked our way through the deserted Mission streets. Christmas trees glowed in the windows. The night air was silent as I waved to him through my open window. I kept wanting him to slow down to avoid a wreck, and the cops. I wondered what they would say. I always try to avoid cops, even on Christmas Eve.

The meter slowly clicked away as we got closer to our destination. I heard a shout from behind. It broke the stillness of my meandering. "Over there!" He was pointing to the middle of a tiny but otherwise ordinary block: Arago Street. We turned the corner, and he remarkably found a spot across the street. He parked without hitting anything and quickly walked toward a house.

He turned to me on the dark sidewalk and said, "Here, come inside, my friend. Thank you." He grinned broadly.

I parked in the driveway and followed him up the stairs.

Before we reached the top, a middle-aged couple flung open the door. They were smiling. I could see pink lights on their tree near the window.

"Thank God you made it, we didn't know what happened," cried the man as he hugged my traveler. He looked at me and said, "Come inside, please." My cab sat silently below, very yellow in the night street light.

"This is my friend, he led me here," said my drunken companion to his friends. "I never would have found you without his help." He turned to me. "Gracias." He shook my hand firmly. It was warm and rough.

"How much do we owe you?" asked the man at the door.

I didn't know what to say. This adventure had cost me about an hour on this busy night, but now it didn't seem so important. I was relieved that it was over, and safely too. "Well, the meter says about $40 . . . but. . . ." I shrugged.

"Oh," said the woman as she looked at the floor. "I, I only have $10, but please come in and we'll feed you. Come inside." She sounded sincere.

I thought about it for a moment. This fare was different. This ride was about more than making money, riding the pulse of the city's, dark streets, and getting from here to there. This man really needed my help, and I rescued him from who knows what. Yet, I still felt that I should go. The woman pulled a $10 bill out of her purse and pushed it at me.

I looked up. "It's okay, the fare's on me. Keep it, I really gotta get back to work." I moved toward the stairs. "Merry Christmas."

"Thank you, thank you sir, and Merry Christmas!" The man and the woman shook my hand and then waved to me as I got back in the cab. Then, laughing, they all went inside and closed the door. I heard their muffled laughter bounce off the curb and dissolve into the quiet night.

I started the engine and chuckled as I turned off the meter. I made my way back to the lonely garage, driving slowly, observing the signs, the stars, the bumps, and the lights. I had seen many strange sights and met many odd and wonderful people while driving the San Francisco streets. This man was another inebriated fare out of thousands, but somehow, he made me feel better about the world, and my little role in it. Maybe I did pick up Jesus on Christmas Eve.

Lousy tipper, but a pretty good guy.

Bob Ecker

More than half the traffic fatalities on Christmas Eve and Christmas Day are alcohol-related, with an average of one death every half-hour.

Learn Ways to Spot a Drunk Driver

If you see a car doing any of the following things, there may be a drunk driver at the wheel.

- Weaving (across center lane, shoulder lane)
- Swerving
- Almost striking a vehicle or other object
- Making unusually wide turns
- Driving without headlights at night
- Driving in opposing lanes or the wrong way on a one-way street
- Showing a slow response to traffic signals (slow start, fast stop)
- Driving substantially below the speed limit
- Accelerating or varying speed for no reason
- Stopping for no apparent reason

If you think you spot a drunk driver, do not attempt to stop the vehicle. Follow from a safe distance and take down the license plate number, description of the vehicle, and the direction in which it is traveling; pull over and call area law enforcement officers.

What You Can You Do to Stop Drunk Driving

- Make a decision to drive responsibly.
- Make a decision never to ride with anyone who has been drinking to the point of impairment.
- Always buckle up—a safety belt is the best protection in a crash.
- Be a responsible drinker.
- Be a responsible party host.
- Be a defensive, alert driver, and report suspected drunk drivers to law enforcement.
- Support efforts to strengthen anti–DUI laws in your state.

If You Are Going Out to Drink

- Designate a driver ahead of time—a designated driver is a non-drinking driver.
- Take a cab or public transportation.
- Make a reservation and spend the night.
- Consume food, sip your drinks, and alternate with nonalcoholic beverages.
- Ask your server about a ride home if you have been drinking to the point of impairment.

If You Are Hosting a Party

- Encourage your guests ahead of time to designate a driver.

- Have a key basket and collect each guest's keys upon arrival. Know the condition of your guests before returning their keys at the end of the party.

- Plan activities so that the focus isn't just on drinking.

- Serve a variety of food and include nonalcoholic beverages alongside alcoholic beverages. The National Commission Against Drunk Driving (www.ncadd.org) can provide nonalcoholic drink recipes.

- If serving punch containing alcohol, mix with a noncarbonated base like a fruit juice; carbonated bases speed up the absorption of alcohol into the blood stream.

- Designate one person to serve as the bartender. This will help control the number of drinks and the amount of alcohol in each drink.

- Stop serving alcohol at least one hour (preferably 90 minutes) before the party is over. Bring out dessert, coffee, and other nonalcoholic drinks.

- Be prepared to arrange for a ride home for your guests if necessary or to invite them to spend the night.

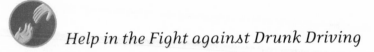

Help in the Fight against Drunk Driving

For further information, check out:

Mothers Against Drunk Driving (MADD):
www.madd.org
Students Against Driving Drunk (SADD):
www.saddonline.com
National Commission Against Drunk Driving
(NCADD): www.ncadd.com

The Mitzvah of Max

The thing we need most is each other.

HUGH MACKAY

On a beautiful California day, Mishkon Tephilo, the small, blue, eighty-year-old synagogue on Main Street in Venice, overflows with worshipers. It's Yom Kippur, a day of penitence and prayer, a time to contemplate failings and omissions, one of only two occasions when Jews neither eat nor drink. And before noon, the sun burnishing the rooftop and the body heat of a standing-room-only crowd turns the sanctuary into an oven.

The Jewish day of atonement, and the holiest day of the year, Yom Kippur fasting begins at sunset and concludes approximately 40 minutes after sunset on the following day.

It is long past midday when Rabbi Naomi Levy delivers her sermon. Looking around the room she recognizes many of the congregants. Notably absent are the congregation's oldest member, Max Polsky, and his wife, Ethyl. Max is ninety-nine, a regular for longer than anyone remembered. In his tenth decade, he has memorized the entire prayer book, as well as special prayers for holidays and festivals. Somewhere in the depths of his memory, clear as a mountain stream, run melodies and chants and the wordless prayers that no one else had ever heard: Max is a living ency-clopedia of prayer. But as he and Ethyl grew feeble, it became more difficult for them to attend services. Now he is in a wheelchair, and it is nearly impossible.

Rabbi Levy puts aside her Yom Kippur sermon, writ-ten and rewritten over weeks, and speaks instead in the moment, from her heart. She tells of the power of prayer to heal, to restore hope, to bring people together. She describes something even more vital than prayer: The imperative to perform *Mitzvot,* good deeds, guideposts on the path to a righteous life. And she relates an ancient *Midrash,* a rabbinical lesson.

"The rabbis of old tell us that a single visit to a sickbed alleviates one-sixtieth of an illness," she says, explaining how people need to feel that they are part of a community, loved and valued. She recalls the story of Joseph going up from Egypt to visit his dying father, Jacob, who was strengthened by the visit. She tells of seeing such a transformation: a cancer patient groaning with pain, invigorated by a visit. In min-utes he was sitting up, taking nourishment, cracking jokes, enjoying life, if only for a while.

Then, looking around the stifling room packed with worshipers hoarse from hours of chanting, weary from stand-ing to pray, suffering the torment of thirst, bellies growling with hunger, clothing heavy with perspiration, and faces flushed from the nearly unbearable heat, Rabbi Levy decides that on this holy day she must ask something from her con-gregation that no one had ever asked before.

"We'll take a break about three," she says. "Services will resume at 4:30. But if you would like to perform a great mitzvah, I invite you to go to Max Polsky's house. Max hasn't missed a Yom Kippur service in over seventy years. He and Ethyl can't come to Mishkon—but maybe we can bring Mishkon to them."

About thirty people tramp more than a mile on sweltering streets to the Polsky home. They bring prayer books and a *shofar*, the ram's horn that recalls God's covenant with Abraham. With Max joining in, the exhausted Mishkonites repeat all the Yom Kippur prayers, from beginning to end. As the cooling evening descends on Venice, blasts from the *shofar* conclude the service.

Bread and wine appear, blessings are quickly chanted, the fast is broken. As Max claps his hands in time to solo renditions of long-forgotten Yiddish folk songs, his blind eyes do not see the joyous tears of his visitors, the community that will not allow him to go alone into darkness. Max seems reborn.

Marvin J. Wolf

Make a Difference in Your Community

- Fix up a youth center or some park benches.
- Donate books and videotapes to the local library.
- Hold a garage sale and donate the money to a local animal rescue shelter.
- Form a Neighborhood Watch program.

- Help repair neglected homes.

- Plant a community garden.

- Give a pint of blood to the local Red Cross blood bank.

- Create a floral arrangement for the local fire or police department. Bring along some coffee and donuts.

- Help out a local farmer's market.

- Have your workplace sponsor a youth sports team and go cheer them on.

Chapter 6

MISSIONS
of the
HEART

All we need to begin with is a dream that we can do better than before. All we need to have is faith, and that dream will come true. All we need to do is act, and the time for action is now.

CARL SANDBURG

Hope for Lora

*Never doubt that a small group of thoughtful,
committed citizens can change the world;
indeed, it's the only thing that ever has.*

Margaret Mead

Lying limply across her grandmother's lap, the child
resembled little more than a rag doll, so still and listless it was hard to tell she was even breathing. Her
name was Lora. She was five. To get her to the rural
Nicaraguan hospital, her *nieta* had first carried Lora for four
miles, passing through a swamp where she tenderly held her
overhead, keeping her high and dry. Then they traveled for
awhile on horseback, took a long bus ride, and walked two
more miles from the bus station to the hospital. There, the
grandmother hoped that a group of Americans could save
the life of the fragile girl she'd carried so far.

I was a part of that group, acting as translator, photographer, and errand runner. The rest of the members were doctors and nurses who had donated eight days of their time to
come to Nicaragua and help as many needy young people
as they could. We were doing so under the auspices of the
Wisconsin Chapter of the all-volunteer organization called
Healing the Children. Word of our impending arrival had
been circulating around the Nicaraguan countryside for
weeks; several intrepid souls, all seeking some type of medical aid, were even waiting for us in the lobby of our airport hotel.

About half the population of Nicaragua lives in poverty, and an estimated 17 percent live in extreme poverty, making Nicaragua one of the poorest countries in Latin America.

The next day we set up our clinic in a rambling, one-story hospital outside the town of Rivas. Stray dogs occasionally trotted down the open-air corridors. Hospital laundry hung out to dry in the branches of nearby trees. In the waiting room, which consisted of nothing more than rows of bare metal folding chairs, sat dozens and dozens of people. Some, like Lora's grandmother, had journeyed for hours, even days, remaining quiet and patient until their turn to be seen by the American doctors. I would frequently pass through this congested waiting area. Every time, I'd find myself the focus of all those pairs of dark brown eyes, each one filled with one word: hope.

The medical team brought with them to Nicaragua much of their own equipment. Nevertheless, they also utilized many local items, trying to ignore the rusty scalpels, the stained, sterile gowns, and the scorpion eggs found in a surgical cabinet. Potential cases were examined carefully. Some children were promptly scheduled for surgery in the next few days and sent off to wait some more in overcrowded wards without air conditioning. There were no complaints. Others, the most difficult cases, could only be helped back in the United States and were put on a different waiting list. Tragically, there were also those who could never be helped. Nicaraguan doctors and nurses worked right alongside the

Americans, both as pupils and as able assistants. By the end of their stay, more than 300 children had been seen and 45 different surgeries performed.

Many of the operations involved facial plastic surgery: removal of tumors, repair of cleft lips and palates. One Nicaraguan mother was frightened by the bandages that wrapped the face of her young son after he was released to her. She was reassured that, once the bandages were removed, he would be the handsomest boy in all the town. Other operations were orthopedic in nature, like that of a young-ster who underwent a double-club-foot procedure. It would allow him to walk normally and to wear shoes for the first time. He left the hospital with a huge entourage of happy relatives surrounding him.

One evening, a dinner in a nearby town was held in our honor. Tables were set up in the backyard of a modest home. Music was provided by some dubious but enthusiastic musi-cians, food was prepared by neighbors, and folks came from all over the village to join in the festivities. The overall feel-ing was one of unity, and the highlight of the night was watching a young woman dance. This pretty girl a few years earlier had herself been helped by some of the same American medical people who were now watching her per-form. Back then she had been weak and frail. And now she was dancing!

By the time that Lora and her grandmother finally made it to the clinic, it was obvious that the child was gravely ill. She was examined almost immediately. Tests proved that she had critical heart problems and, without help, would probably die within a month. Quickly, phone calls were placed to the States to find a heart surgeon and hospital that could accept her on such short notice. Arrangements were then made for her visa and passport, while a foster family was lined up and Lora's airline reservations were made. By the time the team was ready to return to America, miraculously, Lora was able to go with them.

Nine months later I flew to Nicaragua again, this time as an escort for two returning children. One of them was Lora, now an energetic, playful, and healthy girl, not the sick, listless, and barely breathing child of the past.

Her grandmother once again had traveled for hours to meet us. She picked that little girl up in her arms and smothered her with kisses and hugged and hugged her. Then I watched this stoical woman's eyes slowly brim over with tears of joy and relief.

In my heart, I wanted to instantly become a doctor myself and somehow cure all of the sick or injured children I met. But this story is not about what I saw, or what I didn't do. It's about a marvelous yet unassuming group of people: doctors, nurses, mothers and fathers, Nicaraguans and Americans. All were joined together under a common heroic goal. In far-off Nicaragua, they saw—and did.

Jeff Degner

Act Globally and Locally

- For information on international volunteer programs, contact:

  Action Without Borders: www.idealist.org
  International Volunteer Programs Association:
      www.volunteerinternational.org
  The Peace Corps: www.peacecorps.gov
  Volunteers for Peace: www.vfp.org

- Many organizations provide both opportunities
  overseas and projects that are closer to home,
  including:

  Cross-Cultural Solutions:
      www.crossculturalsolutions.org
  Earthwatch Institute: www.earthwatch.org
  National Wildlife Federation: www.nwf.org

Climb for the Cure

*What lies behind us and what lies before us
are tiny matters when compared with
what lies within us.*

RALPH WALDO EMERSON

I took a step. Three breaths later, I took another. At more than 20,000 feet above sea level, within a geological stone's throw of the Arctic Circle, the available oxygen was about one-half of what I had been breathing just a few weeks earlier at my college graduation. The winds were gusting at more than 50 miles an hour, lowering the temperature to 40 degrees. Visibility was rapidly diminishing. Through fogged goggles I could almost see what I knew was only a few hundred yards away—the highest point in North America, the summit of Denali.

Denali ("The High One") is the Native American word for North America's highest peak, now known as Mount McKinley, at 20,320 feet.

For two years, I had marked this point as the symbolic height of what I could achieve. As the winds picked up and I struggled to remain standing, I began to realize what I had never believed possible. Now, within 200 yards of the top, it was too dangerous for my team to continue. I bellowed. I screamed. I gasped. And I turned around.

As my mind adjusted to the idea of descent, I thought back to why I was up there in the first place.

I thought back to when I was eleven years old and my best friend Robbie's mother contracted AIDS from a blood transfusion and later died.

I thought back to the years that followed, years where I had grown from a little boy to a man, and in the process came to realize that AIDS represented a major challenge to my generation.

I thought back to the summer before my junior year, in Washington State's North Cascades, when it occurred to me that climbing was a fitting metaphor for the fight against AIDS—by taking one step at a time, you could achieve the impossible. Climb for the Cure was born.

With our summit attempt aborted, we stumbled down the mountain's steep ice, pointing our crampons in the direction of our camp some 3,000 feet below. All of us were deeply exhausted. At the top of a particularly difficult section of the descent, we switched around the order of our rope team.

I felt fairly strong, so I moved to the back. If someone fell on this steep section, I figured that I could hold them in self-arrest. The visibility was very poor, and my mind felt detached, floating back to the summit ridge, replaying our failed attempt.

I forced myself to concentrate on the situation at hand. Where was my ice axe? It was in my downhill hand. *Pay attention, Alex!* I grabbed it with my other hand and focused on fitting my crampons into the narrow-cut ice steps that traversed the 45-degree pass.

Sometime later I realized that my teammate in front had forgotten to clip the safety line that extended behind him and connected to me—the running belay was no longer a belay.

We are at our limit, I thought. Our safety margin has disappeared. We had given all we could, and we had failed.

We made it back to our high camp and collapsed into our tents. Lying there, I kept thinking this couldn't be it. This wasn't the way it was supposed to be.

I was firmly determined to make the project a national example of what a group of students could do in the fight against AIDS. From Wall Street to Washington to colleges around the country, we had spread the message. We had raised the research money, in-kind services, and media space. All that remained was to climb the mountain.

I awoke the morning after our failed attempt to a terrible sense of dread. The winds that had battered us near the summit had descended to our high camp, where they remained. Each day I hoped the next would bring clear weather and a chance to try for the summit one more time. Our tasks were minimal: maintain the ice walls we had built to shelter our tents, keep ourselves hydrated and fed, and rest.

On the third day of the storm, two other climbing expeditions camped near us abandoned their summit plans. In a wonderfully touching gesture, they gave us their food, enabling us to keep waiting.

"Bless you for what you are doing," one said.

I watched him begin his long, lonely descent, praying

that when I followed him it would be after having done what we had set out to do.

But the storm remained, and after five days above 17,000 feet, my team and I were physically wasted. On the fifth night, I knew we could not stay much longer.

I was unable to sleep that night, and then, around 4:00 A.M., the winds died down. My team and I roused ourselves and looked upward. There was only whiteness and disorientation.

I tried to give an encouraging talk, and it felt hollow, partly from exhaustion, but mostly from fear—fear that we would set out once again for the summit and fail, or that one or more of us might get hurt. And yet we had never wanted anything more in our lives.

We started climbing.

A thousand feet above, the winds picked up dramatically, and three in the group decided to turn back. Physically they had nothing left and could not go on. With tears in her eyes, Annie, one of my closest friends, hugged me and whispered in my ear, "Angels will carry the rest of you upward."

We continued climbing.

The weather got worse, and I started to feel ill. I wasn't sure if it was physical or emotional, and I knew it didn't matter. I would not turn back. Not now. Not ever. Visibility was only a few feet and the ice was steep, but the route felt like it had rails. We knew where to go.

Step by step we headed to the top. We traversed past steep ice slopes and a giant crevasse known as Jaws. At 19,000 feet, we climbed across the upper reaches of the mountain.

Visibility was deteriorating rapidly, and I felt a combination of great fear and great determination—a feeling of being very much alive and in the moment. We made our way across a relatively flat plateau, about 500 feet below the summit, known as the "football field."

The ice slope to the peak loomed above us. We were drawing on energy we didn't even know we had. Step. Three breaths. Another step. And another and another. And then, at last, one final step.

In an early evening of mountain whiteness after two years of planning, one month of climbing, and so much dreaming, five Climb for the Cure members wept on the summit of North America.

Alex Friedman

 ## *Work for a Cause Close to Your Heart*

Ask yourself these questions:

- What are you passionate about? (Preferably something from your own life or that of someone you know)

- What are your special talents?

- Do you want to work with an established organization or start one of your own?

- How much time can you give?

- Who can you think of that might be interested in working with you or offering advice?

- What is your first step?

The Old Rusty Key

*Giving of ourselves is the way we change the
world at the end of our fingertips.*

RICHARD F. SCHUBERT

I t was a cool September morning when we piled into the
dilapidated university van. The group of fifteen college
students that I was leading was heading to Milwaukee
to help build homes in a poor inner city neighborhood with
Habitat for Humanity.

> Habitat for Humanity has built more than 150,000 houses
> around the world, providing more than 750,000 people in
> more than 3,000 communities with safe, decent, affordable
> shelter. The cost of Habitat houses varies from as little as
> $800 in some developing countries to an average of $46,600
> in the United States.

When we arrived on the site, I found the construction
supervisor and told him that we wanted to tackle the tough-
est job on the site. He smiled and led us to the backyard to
an enormous pile of debris and said, "I figure that this pile
was here before any of you were born. I'd like to chuck it
all in the Dumpster out front."

We named the pile "Mount Habitat" and began the ardu-
ous task of shoveling the debris into wheelbarrows and lug-

ging it to the Dumpster. About two hours into our work, several children from the community walked over and began to watch us. We invited them to join us in our mountain assault, and they enthusiastically agreed.

The smallest boy of the group hung back as the other children put on gloves and began to work. I was working on a far corner of the pile, and I smiled at him when he glanced my way. He strode up to me, puffed out his chest, and stated, "My name's J.T. and I'm real strong."

"Well, I can see that," I replied. "My name is David and I really need some help." I grabbed a shovel that was nearby and handed it to my small helper.

The shovel towered over him by a full two feet, and his tiny hands couldn't even wrap around the handle. Without a moment's hesitation he dug into the pile with great passion. Every few minutes he would stop, look up at me, and exclaim with pride, "I'm helping."

And each time I responded, "I don't know what we would do without you, J.T."

He was dressed much like the other kids: blue jeans rolled up at the bottom so he could grow into them, a T-shirt dirty from the day's adventures, and an unbuttoned, well-worn red-and-white flannel. He wore high-top basketball shoes that were purposely left untied, and upon closer inspection I realized that they were two different shoes.

But it was his beautiful brown eyes that set him apart. When he smiled, his eyes remained wide open, which forced his cheeks to bulge out like the cheeks of a cherub. I tried to imagine what this little boy would look like when the rest of his frail body caught up with his eyes.

While J.T. and I worked, we shared stories with each other. He told me about his mom and dad, his sisters, and his neighborhood. I told him stories about my family and school.

In order to amuse each other, we took turns making up stories about items that we found in the pile. A rusted hubcap became a gear from a flying saucer that crashed many years ago. A beat-up old shoe and a broken cup were transformed into a priceless modern art exhibit. I found an old rusted skeleton key and created a story about a magic space ship. When I finished telling the story, I gave J.T. the key and said, "Now you have the magic key that starts that space ship."

He gazed at me with those huge brown eyes and then ran over to his friends to show them his new treasure.

J.T. and I worked side by side the entire day. I had to give up my shovel a few times when some of the adult volunteers needed one, but I always made sure that my new friend had his orange-handled shovel.

And then, as we were getting ready to quit for the day, a well-dressed elderly man walking with a cane called one of the children over. The man then began to yell, "Unless you're gettin' paid, you git away from there and go home right now. I mean it, right now."

All of the children dropped their shovels and quickly dispersed. A woman from our group approached the man and tried to explain Habitat for Humanity's philosophy to him. He was unfamiliar with Habitat's work and refused to believe that people would volunteer their time and then sell the home for no profit. He turned away and continued to shout to the children.

I watched J.T. as he scurried off. He slowed and seemed suspended between the urgings of his peers, the commands of the elderly man, and our group. I stood silently clutching my shovel. He turned and his eyes found mine. We shared a mutual smile. Again, he ran toward his friends, but then he stopped, turned around, and ran back toward me.

He grasped my hand and pulled me down so that we were eye to eye. Standing on his tiptoes, he whispered in my ear, "You'll always be my friend." Then he pressed something into my hand and ran off with the other children.

I never saw J.T. again, but I will always treasure the gift that he gave me: the old rusty key to his magic space ship.

David Guzzetta

Participate in Existing Community Projects

Contact a local nonprofit organization.

- To find an organization, look in a local phone book under the organization's name. Visit its Web site or call. Some examples of nonprofit organizations are food banks, animal rescue leagues, homeless shelters, and faith-based programs.

- The Corporation for National and Community Service provides information on nonprofit organizations in your community (www.nationalservice.org).

- Contact the local Rotary Club. The Rotary Club database has numerous ideas for projects that will benefit the community (www.rotary.org).

- To search by location for additional volunteer programs, check out: www.volunteermatch.org.

- Other well-known national service groups are the following:

  Boys and Girls Clubs of America: www.bgca.org
  Red Cross: www.redcross.org
  Teach for America: www.teachforamerica.org

- Take part in an existing fund-raising event, such as:

  AIDS Walk: www.aidswalk.net
  Great Strides, a 10K walk sponsored by the Cystic
     Fibrosis Foundation, to cure cystic fibrosis:
     www.cff.org
  MS Walk, for the National Multiple Sclerosis
     Society: www.nationalmssociety.com
  Race for the Cure: www.komen.org

Lura Lake

The day will come when I will die.
So the only consequence before me is
what I will do with my allotted time.
I can remain on shore, paralyzed with fear, or
I can raise my sails and dip and soar in the breeze.

RICHARD BODE

ob Brush had cancer and a dream. The doctor had given Bob six months to live. Bob's dream was to clean up Lura Lake, a 1,200-acre body of water located in Blue Earth County, Minnesota. Thanks mostly to the work of carp creating an underwater pasture, Lura Lake had become a brown prairie lake.

The Great Lakes contain 20 percent of the world's surface water. Only 1 percent of the Great Lakes water is renewed each year.

Many things catch our eyes, but few catch our hearts. Bob gave his heart to Lura Lake. Bob would be the first to admit that he could not have accomplished anything without the help of countless others, but Bob Brush was the driving force. He raised money by selling sweatshirts and asking for donations. He formed the Lura Lake Association. A chemical treatment was applied to the lake to kill the carp. Riprap was put in spots along the shoreline where erosion was a problem. Willow trees and native grasses were planted among the rock. A network of cable and logs was installed to prevent further erosion of treed shoreline.

Much of the work in revitalizing the lake was done by volunteers. Schoolchildren volunteered their efforts to plant trees. Two aeration units were installed on Lura Lake, and it was stocked with game fish. Within three years, people were catching good-sized perch, walleye, and northern pike. The water clarity has become so good that I am told a pair of common loons nested and raised their young on Lura Lake last year.

Lura Lake just held its seventh annual Lura Lake Fair—birdwatching, teaching kids how to fish, beekeeping, programs by the Raptor Center, and pontoon rides were just a few of the featured events. I talked to a number of fishermen who were very happy. Things are going well at Lura Lake, and it all started with a dream that Bob Brush had ten years ago.

What will Bob do now?

Plenty. He's working on four other lakes in the area. Yes, ten years ago, Bob Brush had a dream and cancer. His dream is coming true. As to the cancer, his doctor has told him that whatever he is doing, he'd better keep right on doing it.

Al Batt

Become Active in Projects to Protect, Preserve, and Save the Environment

There are many environmental issues that need your help:

- Protecting habitats and various species of animals
- Saving forests, lakes, wild lands, and parks
- Preventing global warming
- Clean water and ocean campaigns
- Clean air and energy campaigns

If you feel passionately about one of these issues, you can get started by:

- Raising awareness of the problem in your area by using flyers, road signs, press releases, and newspaper articles.
- Recruiting a group of interested people who will spearhead the project with you, or look to various environmental organizations for assistance in getting your project attention and funding.

As a start, check out these organizations:

Earth Justice: ww.earthjustice.org
Natural Resources Defense Council: www.nrdc.org
National Wildlife Federation: www.nwf.org
Save Our Environment:
    www.saveourenvironment.org
Sierra Club: www.sierraclub.org
World Wildlife Fund: www.worldwildlife.org

A Winning Smile

I expect to pass through this life but once.
If therefore, there can be any kindness I can show,
or any good thing I can do to a fellow human being,
let me do it now.

WILLIAM PENN

On a normal weekday, Nicholas Marriam would bound home from school with a sunny smile, eager to discuss his day with his mom and eat a snack. Energetic and fun, the blond-haired boy from Edgewater, Maryland, was like most second graders: he enjoyed frolicking with friends, playing games, and hatching ambitious plans.

He loved school and his teachers, and he beamed with pride when showing off his new baby brother, Alex, just six months old.

But on Friday, October 1, 1999, Nick came home feeling less than his happy-go-lucky self. Exhausted and short of breath, he headed to bed for what he thought would be a short nap. Nick's short nap lasted through dinner and the night. The next day, he wasn't interested in breakfast, or a lunch outing to Chuck E. Cheese's. When Nick told his mother, Angel, that he didn't want to go outside at all because it hurt to breathe, she became alarmed. By Saturday evening his condition had worsened, and she drove him to a hospital emergency room in Annapolis, not far from their home.

At the ER, Nick inhaled doses of asthma medicine, but his condition didn't improve. The staff thought Nick suffered from a reactive airway brought on by allergies or a cold. But Angel couldn't shake a feeling that something was wrong. She insisted that Nick receive a chest X-ray.

By 2:00 A.M., Nick had been to radiology and was resting. Angel headed to a pay phone to make a call. But as she walked by an exam room, she overheard a chilling conversation no mother wants to hear:

"We'll need ten copies of this. Everyone will want to look at it," an X-ray technician told a colleague.

"That poor little boy," the other replied.

Captured in blinding white on the X-ray was a massive tumor. It pushed at Nick's chest cavity, shoving his heart under his armpit. One lung had collapsed; the other labored to do its job. Nick, just four weeks shy of his seventh birthday, had cancer: T-cell lymphoma, a rarity in children.

Within twenty-four hours, Nick traveled to Children's Hospital in Washington, D.C., where he underwent surgery. Chemotherapy began with the first of thousands of intravenous drips. His parents stayed at his bedside—one of 172 nights they'd spend that first year in the hospital. Relying on family and friends to take care of Alex, they stayed to sleep with their son, to massage his weak limbs when he cried out in pain, and to hold his bedpan when he was sick from the chemicals that worked on the disease but poisoned his body. They watched his golden hair fall out on his pillow, yet marveled as his smile endured.

Throughout the surgeries and endless hospital stays, Nick fought the cancer. Looking back, he says he never really considered he might die; he just wore a smile because he hated seeing his mother—and fellow patients—sad.

Often, when he was well enough, he would visit with some of the other kids in the hospital, trying his best to cheer them up. Nick went to the other patients' rooms to tell jokes, play board games, and chat.

By the following summer of 2000, Nick was able to attend Camp Friendship in Laytonsville, Maryland, a getaway for pediatric cancer patients. He enjoyed the camaraderie and the shared experiences, and the camp worked wonders to rekindle his playful personality.

A year later, he returned to Camp Friendship, where a counselor suggested that campers channel their energy and good spirit into volunteerism. The counselor told Nick about *USA WEEKEND's* Make A Difference Day, a national day of volunteering.

In 2003, 3 million people cared enough about their communities to volunteer on Make A Difference Day, accomplishing thousands of projects in hundreds of towns.

Nick wanted to learn more. When his mother picked him up at the camp, he told her about it and discussed his idea for a project: He ached to help families back at Children's Hospital's pediatric oncology ward.

He remembered seeing his mother cry when a friend brought her a gift basket containing soap and shampoo. She never packed a bag for Nick's hospital appointments, hoping it would bring good luck. As much as she knew that she was going to spend time at the hospital, she didn't want to jinx herself, and Nick, by packing an overnight bag.

That moment made a lasting impression on Nick. For Make A Difference Day, he chose to collect toiletries, food, and dining gift certificates to give to ill kids and their exhausted parents. He discussed his project with everyone he met, explaining how he planned to make a difference for these kids and their parents. By October 27, 2001—Make A Difference Day, and two years after Nick's initial diagnosis—he'd collected $7,500 worth of merchandise for 166 gift bags. Together with his parents, an aunt, and nine-year-old cousin Shelby, Nick delivered the bags and a meal to each of the parents on the ward.

"I remember my mom would always eat junk out of the vending machines. She never got a good meal. The hospital has a cafeteria, but it's expensive and the parents have to worry about money. I wanted them to have food," Nick said shortly after his first Make A Difference Day project.

The bags were a welcome surprise, but more notewor-thy—at least for the parents—were Nick's energy, enthusi-asm, and health. This little boy was a manifestation of their hopes. Just one look, one smile, one handshake, and they could see that some children do beat the deadly disease.

In 2002, Nick was recognized by *USA WEEKEND Magazine* for his charitable project as one of ten national Make A Difference Day honorees. He continues the proj-ect annually, having extended it to two hospitals—Children's and Duke University Hospital—since moving to Clayton, North Carolina, that same year. He continues to spread his good cheer, telling oncology patients he wants to be a scientist and find a cancer cure. He also talks about his alternate career choice—one that would capitalize on his winning smile and already fine-tuned bedside matter—a pediatric oncologist.

Marcia L. Bullard

Participate in USA WEEKEND's Make A Difference Day

Make A Difference Day, the national day of doing good, is an annual event that takes place on the fourth Saturday in October. Sponsored by *USA WEEKEND Magazine* in partnership with the Points of Light Foundation, Make A Difference Day is supported by actor Paul Newman, who donates $10,000 each to ten selected Make A Difference Day projects.

- Ask what your community needs. Are people hungry, homeless, or ill? Are parks or schools dirty or neglected? No matter where you live, there's a need nearby. You can act alone or enlist your friends, family, and coworkers. If you need inspiration or ideas to get you started, check out the Idea Generator at: www.makeadifferenceday.com.

- To see what others have done through the years and for more information, visit: www.makeadifferenceday.com or call 1-800-416-3824.

Amazing Maisie

In every community there is work to be done.
In every nation, there are wounds to heal.
In every heart, there is the power to do it.

MARIANNE WILLIAMSON

Back in 1973, there were only two swimming spots near Maisie DeVore's home in Eskridge, Kansas. The first was Lake Wabaunsee, which was filled with Canada geese, and the second was a pool in Alma, about 25 miles away. Maisie wanted something better for her two young children and her community. But the town's population of 500 didn't have the money for a pool, so she vowed to come up with the money—one can, one jam, one penny at a time.

Maisie began driving weekly routes through the city and around Wabaunsee County collecting aluminum cans, scrap metals, and car batteries plus all sorts of other junk before hauling it to a scrap metal recycling center in Topeka, where she sold it. When their appliances stopped working, local residents took them over to Maisie to be resold for scrap. She also hawked her own homemade crab apple jelly and raffled off afghans that she had hand-knitted. Maisie did this for thirty years, and, after collecting and selling more than 6 million soda cans, she was now in her early eighties and had raised more than $73,000 on her own.

"That may not sound like much," she said, "but that's how we got to this point—small amounts at a time."

Then, the state presented Maisie with a matching check for $73,000. Others kicked in as well with private donations. An anonymous Topeka business sent $12,000. The Flint Hills Bank of Eskridge gave $5,000. Strangers mailed checks, big and small. Even actress Glenn Close sent $2,000 when she was shooting three made-for-television movies in the area. In fact, as Maisie herself explained, "I won a part as an extra in all three productions, after reading a casting call in the newspaper for 'weathered farm faces.'"

The school board donated some land for the pool beside Eskridge Elementary School. Maisie's picture window overlooked the school, where two of her own children had graduated when it was still a high school.

Finally, in the spring of 2001, Maisie used a shovel her grandson had painted gold the night before to turn over two heaps of soil where the pool would be located. Dayton, Maisie's six-and-a-half-year-old great-grandson, seemed a little perplexed by the ceremonial groundbreaking.

"She's just gonna dig that puny little hole?" he asked, wondering why his great-grandmother wouldn't singlehandedly dig the entire pool with her golden shovel. "Just two scoops?"

"He may not have been too far off," said Eskridge's Mayor. "Once Maisie and I start shoveling, watch out, because we might not straighten up until that thing's dug."

Less than four months later, on July 14, more than 1,000 people attended a parade honoring both the opening of Maisie's Community Swimming Pool and one very determined great-grandmother of nine.

There are more than 14,000 year-round, full-size pools in 8,058 communities and 133 countries around the world.

"If you think you can't do something, you probably can't," said Maisie. "But when I think I can, one way or another, I get it done."

The pool itself can hold more than one-fifth of the town, and over the decades, its visionary came to be known as Amazing Maisie.

"A guy was kidding me and he said, 'We're going to get you a bikini and you're going to be the first one in.'" Maisie said, before adding with a smile, "I doubt it. Some kid will beat me to it."

I'm not so sure about that.

Steve Zikman

Remember the Words of Arthur Ashe:

"Start where you are. Use what you have. Do what you can."

Afterword

A FEW YEARS AGO, my wife and I brought some Christmas gifts to a struggling family in the southeast part of Washington, D.C. Over time, we got to know two of the children and started mentoring them.

The younger brother, Kevin, was small but energetic. While he was always smiling broadly, his older brother, Roy, was very sullen and reserved. We met with them almost every week. They would often spend the weekend with my wife and me. When we couldn't get together, we'd speak over the phone. They became a part of our family.

Over the years, both brothers learned that they get out of life what they bring to it. Kevin is now much better at setting goals, and Roy has become more confident, more joyful, and more focused as he has moved from adolescence to adulthood.

Somehow, we have found a way to light two precious candles.

I read not long ago about a man in his early fifties who traveled each day by bus to a home where he spent every afternoon with a seven-year-old boy who was blind, speechless, and profoundly retarded. When interviewed by the local newspaper about his motivation for doing this, the man said simply, "He can't walk. He can't talk. He can't see. This boy needs me."

While this was a wonderful example of volunteering, it was made even more special by the fact that the man himself was mildly retarded, had cerebral palsy, and needed two canes in order to walk. Fate had given him a whole list of excuses for not getting involved, as well as reasons to feel sorry for himself, to turn an eye from the plight and pain of others.

Instead, this remarkable soul chose another path. He chose to do something right for someone else. He chose to volunteer. And every time he sat with the boy, he did what no government agency, well-endowed private institution, or mighty corporation could do. He touched and transformed another human life with the miracle of affirmation and love.

Whose responsibility is it to introduce light and life, meaning and joy, into the lives of others?

It is not government alone, although government has an indispensable role to perform. It is not the churches and synagogues, although they might be the wellspring of that conviction. It is not large organizations and companies, although they too play a critical part in amassing the resources and extending the services to those who need it.

It is the responsibility of every single individual. Whether spending time with a child, tending to the sick, planting a tree, or reaching out to someone in need of a gentle touch, we all share some of the responsibility.

Some years back, my wife and I hosted a young Japanese student who was a part of a program that brought students to America. One day, I noticed a brown paper bag filled with trash sitting on my front porch. I didn't know how it got there and disposed of it. Two days later, I found another brown paper bag and, with each passing day, yet another. And another. I came to learn that this young man, a visitor in our country, would collect trash along the side of the road as he walked from the bus stop to our home.

I was reminded of the words of Helen Keller: "The world is moved not only by the mighty shoves of the heroes, but also by the aggregate of the tiny pushes of each honest worker."

Indeed, let each of us do our part. Let each of us be an honest worker. Let each of us light a candle and do some good . . . for goodness' sake.

Robert K. Goodwin
President and CEO,
The Points of Light Foundation

Share Your Stories

WE INVITE YOU TO SEND us your own "Doing Good" stories.

To do so, please visit our Web site at:
www.GOscape.com

Acknowledgments

I WISH TO EXPRESS MY GRATITUDE TO:

My family for their soft words and open hearts, especially Rob, my parents Thelma and Joel, Sandra and Desmond, Susan, Janice, Steven, Revo, Barbie, and Lea.

My Hawaiian family at Inner Ocean Publishing, especially John Elder, Karen Bouris, Mark Kerr, Alma Bune, Heather McArthur, Pam Suwinsky, and Suzanne Albertson. You have brought joy, caring, and enthusiasm to the creative process.

My team of inspired interns: Cara Cassidy, Carsten Cheung, Cyndy Glucksman, Alice Han, Jeanie Kim, Linda Kim, and Sunmin Lee.

All of the book's contributors, who have so graciously blazed a path for doing good.

Contributors

Amelia Ashford–Phillips resides in Florida and has one son. She has worked in the Florida state prison system and, in 1998, retired from social work at a north Florida VA medical center. She now enjoys cooking, writing, and gardening with her husband.

Rosalie J. Bakken, Ph.D., grew up in Lake Mills, Iowa, and attended Iowa State University and Drake University. She is passionate about making the world a better place for youth and future generations. Her primary inspiration is her daughter. Rosalie can be reached at Rosalie@Zorabella.com.

Al Batt is a writer, speaker, humorist, and storyteller who lives in rural Hartland, Minnesota. He loves what he does and loves where he does it. He is a newspaper columnist, TV and radio personality, and an avid birder. He may be reached at SnoEowl@aol.com.

Harry Belafonte is well known worldwide for his accomplishments as both a performer and a humanitarian. He has achieved great fame as a recording artist, concert singer, actor and producer on Broadway, and is a strong advocate for human rights. In 1985, Mr. Belafonte brought together 45 top performers to record the song 'We Are the World', which raised millions of dollars for emergency assistance in Africa. On 4 March 1987, he was appointed UNICEF Goodwill Ambassador. In May 1997, Belafonte was honoured by the United Nations for his work on behalf of children around the world. At the ceremony, he was presented with the UNICEF Silver Statuette to commemorate 10 years as UNICEF Goodwill Ambassador.

Heather Black's stories of love, miracles, and guardian angels appear regularly in the pages of *Woman's World* magazine.

Dr. Mike Bradshaw is a state extension specialist with K-State Research and Extension. He serves as a health and safety support staff to county extension educators in the 105 counties of the state. He has been with the Extension service for the past 26 years.

Stephanie Ray Brown of Henderson, Kentucky, enjoys writing daily ditties about her childhood and raising children Savannah and Cameron along with husband Terry's help. She gets tickled each and every time a story so near and dear to her heart touches another.
She can be reached at savvysdad@aol.com.

Marcia L. Bullard is president and chief executive officer of *USA WEEKEND Magazine*, the national Sunday newspaper magazine. *USA WEEKEND,* with 50 million readers, is distributed in 600 newspapers nationwide. *USA WEEKEND* creates Make A Difference Day in 1992; it is the nation's largest day of volunteering. Ms. Bullard serves on the boards of directors of the Points of Light Foundation and America's Charities. She is a member of the Newspaper Association of America, the American Society of Newspaper Editors, and the Association of Educators in Journalism and Mass Communications. A native of Springfield, Illinois, Ms. Bullard lives in Washington, D.C., with her husband, Tom McNamara, and has a stepdaughter, Emily.

Sandra J. Campbell is a published author who resides in Garden City, Michigan, with her husband, Michael. She is also delighted to be one of ThreeOlBags, a trio of travel writers who visit, photograph, and write articles about people and places of interest in their Great Lake State and beyond!
Web site: www.threeolbags.com.

Nicole Christie has been writing since age seven, when she penned her first short story, "Nancy the Nanny Goat." She now spends her days as a corporate communications writer and also writes on a freelance basis for magazines and newspapers. Samples of her work can be viewed at: www.nicolechristie.com.

D.D. Cummings lives in the Midwest, where he is currently working on his first novel. He was a 2002 runner-up in the online Galleria Eros Short Fiction Awards. Two of his short stories will be published in the anthology *Tales of the Unknown,* edited by Stephen M. T. Greene (Spring 2004).

Lynne Daroff is a freelance writer, political activist, and grandmother . . . not necessarily in that order. You can write her at LynneDaroff@aol.com.

Jeff Degner lives in Barrington, Illinois, with his wife, Marcie, and dog, Charm. A customer service agent for Delta Airlines at O'Hare for more than thirty years, he also volunteers as the travel and escort coordinator for the Wisconsin and Illinois chapters of Healing the Children.
His e-mail is j.degner@sbcglobal.net.

The Eastern Ontario Poverty Resource Network promotes information sharing on strategies, best practices, research, community development initiatives, self-help and other resources regarding child poverty. The Network is a project of the Social Planning Council of Ottawa, Canada. Please visit their website at www.spottawa.on.ca/EOCPRN.

Bob Ecker is a Napa, California–based freelance writer, covering travel, food, and wine for a variety of publications, including the *Boston Globe, Dallas Morning News,* and *San Francisco Chronicle.* His taxi stories are behind him, yet fondly remembered. He can be reached at bvp3@mindspring.com.

Karen E. Eifler taught middle school students for ten years. Since 1998 she has worked on preparing the next generation of teachers, working as a professor of education at the University of Portland, Oregon. Son Conor and husband Mark provide the goodness in her life. Talk to her via e-mail at eifler@up.edu.

Dr. Mickey Eisenberg is a professor of medicine at the University of Washington and Medical Program Director of the King County EMS system.
His e-mail is gingy@u.washington.edu.

Susan Farr Fahncke is the author of *Angel's Legacy* and the coauthor of and contributor to numerous other books. Susan also runs Angels2TheHeart, a foundation that sends care packages and cards to critically ill people. She lives in Utah and teaches online writing workshops. Visit her Web site at www.2TheHeart.com.

FamilyEducationNetwork is the Internet's leading network of sites providing education-based solutions to parents (www.FamilyEducation.com), kids (www.FunBrain.com), and teachers (www.TeacherVision.com). Parents are provided with practical guidance, grade-specific information about their children's school experience, strategies to get involved with their children's learning, free e-mail newsletters, and fun and entertaining family activities.

Rick Fico was born and raised in Chicago and now lives in Las Vegas. Rick is an aspiring writer whose pen still points in the direction of the strongest wind. He is currently writing his memoir while pursuing other challenges. He loves to travel and learn from others. You can e-mail him at rickjfico@yahoo.com.

For Love of Children (FLOC) has been at the forefront of family-centered child welfare reform in Washington, D.C., since 1965. FLOC programs identify and build on strengths in children and their families. FLOC equips children with the tools and motivation they need to escape the cycle of poverty, homelessness, and educational failure that has afflicted previous generations, so they may reach their full potential. Please visit For Love of Children at www.floc.org or contact (202) 462-8686.

Alex Friedman lives in New York City, where he works as an investment banker at Lazard. Alex served as a White House Fellow in the Clinton Administration and as an assistant to the Secretary of Defense. He holds a J.D./M.B.A. from Columbia and a B.A. from Princeton. Alex is an active mountaineer and rock climber and has participated in major climbing expeditions throughout South America, Alaska, and Asia. You may contact him at alex.friedman@lazard.com.

Ryan Furer lives in Chicago and has been working in the field of experiential education since receiving a degree in Recreation, Parks, and Tourism Administration from Western Illinois University in 1991. His hobbies include rock climbing, golf, playing guitar, listening to live music, and spreading the word about Wilson's disease.

Robert K. Goodwin is the president and CEO of the Points of Light Foundation. Goodwin was instrumental in the development of the 1997 Presidents' Summit for America's Future, which celebrated a commitment to improve the quality of life for this nation's youth. He created Connect America, a collaborative effort led by the Points of Light Foundation, the Corporation for National Service, and a diverse group of national and local organizations—nonprofits, civic associations, local governments, businesses, labor unions, fraternal organizations, and news media—to engage every American in helping to solve serious social and community problems through volunteering. The *NonProfit Times* also selected him for six years in a row as one of the fifty most influential people in the nonprofit sector.

David Guzzetta is a carpenter, traveler, writer, and snappy dresser. When not cooking gourmet meals, he enjoys biking and long beach walks with his faithful companion, Kyma. He is still trying to write the great American novel or at least a publishable kid's story.
He occasionally checks his e-mail at guzzu22@hotmail.com.

Joan Halperin writes prose, essays, and poetry. She teaches creative writing in schools, hospitals, and prisons and has taught in battered women's centers. She has been published in *Midnight Mind, Rosebud, ByLine, Cimmaron Review, Tar River Poetry,* and several anthologies. She lives and works in Canton, Massachusetts.

Cynthia M. Hamond has been writing for six years. She has numerous stories in Multnomah's *Stories for the Heart* series as well as the *Chicken Soup for the Soul* series and in magazines. She has received three writing recognitions and her story, "Goodwill" is a TV favorite. You may e-mail her at Candbh@aol.com.

Laura Hogg has worked at Starlight Children's Foundation Canada (www.starlightcanada.org) for fourteen years and, for the past five, has served as its executive director. Starlight is an international nonprofit organization dedicated to brightening the lives of seriously ill children through wish granting and other entertainment-related activities. Laura is the mother of three stepchildren and a newborn son, Matthew.

Laurel Holliday is the author of the *Children of Conflict* series (Pocket Books/Simon & Schuster), which explores growing up in regions of cultural conflict and violence such as Northern Ireland and Israel/Palestine. She is a psychotherapist, freelance journalist, and online educator.
She can be reached at laurelholl@comcast.net.

Bertamae Anger Ives, M.S., is the mother of two sons. She is an organist and former public school teacher. One of her hobbies is collecting antiques. Currently, she and her brother, Dr. Dan Anger, are working on a book called *Claim Happiness Now.* Her e-mail address is auntbertieanger@cs.com.

Brenda Jank is captivated by the ordinary and extraordinary stories of life. She's a dedicated storyteller, sharing stories of love and grace in a world desiring a touch from God. A Christian author and national speaker, Brenda lives near Ft. Wayne, Indiana, and can be reached via e-mail at brenda@lutherhaven.org.

Kids Can Make A Difference® is an innovative educational program for middle school and high school students. It helps them understand the root causes of hunger and poverty and how they—as individuals—can take action. For further information, visit their Web site at www.kidscanmakeadifference.org.

Rabbi Charles A. Kroloff was the spiritual leader for thirty-six years of New Jersey's largest synagogue, Temple Emanu-El of Westfield. A past president of the Central Conference of American Rabbis, the organization of Reform rabbis worldwide, he is the author of *When Elijah Knocks: A Religious Response to Homelessness,* published by Behrman House.

Beth Levine is a freelance writer whose work has appeared in *Reader's Digest, Family Circle, Redbook, Lifetime, Good Housekeeping,* and *Woman's Day,* among others. She is the author of *Divorce: Young People Caught in the Middle* and *Playgroups: A Complete Guide for Parents.* She lives in Stamford, Connecticut.

Hayley Linfield currently lives and works in Toronto, Ontario, Canada. A part-time ESL teacher, she has published her writing appeared in a variety of print and online literary journals. She can be reached at helinfield@yahoo.ca.

Elisabet McHugh was born and raised in Sweden. She lives in Idaho.

Laura Laemmle Meehan was a senior editor at FamilyEducationNetwork, a Web site for parents of little kids, big kids, and teenagers. She lives in Winchester, Massachusetts, and has two teens of her own, Samantha and Max. Her e-mail address is lmeehan61@comcast.net.

Dr. Robert Myers is a child psychologist and is founder of the Child Development Institute, which provides information for parents at www.cdipage.com. He has twenty years of experience in private practice and has provided parent education on radio and magazines.

The National Commission Against Drunk Driving (NCADD) is the successor organization to the Presidential Commission on Drunk Driving appointed by President Ronald Reagan in 1982 at the behest of a bipartisan Congress. The Presidential Commission developed the first national report on this issue, along with comprehensive recommendations for reducing alcohol-impaired driving in America. The National Commission works to continue the efforts of the President's Commission to focus the nation on ways to reduce this most serious public health and safety problem. For further information, go to www.NCADD.com.

Prevent Child Abuse America is the leading organization working at the national, state, and local levels to prevent the abuse and neglect of our nation's children. Headquartered in Chicago, Prevent Child Abuse America has a network of chapters in thirty-nine states and is known for its public awareness campaigns, prevention programs, advocacy efforts, and research. For more information on how you can prevent child abuse and neglect, please visit www.preventchildabuse.org.

Marcia Reed is a freelance writer and photographer, specializing in travel, folk art, and cultural history. Her stories and photos on Mexican colonial cities have appeared in the *Los Angeles Times* special sections. Her stories and photos of international folk art (Malaysian, German, Norwegian, and French) have been published in several magazines.

Ferris Robinson is the mother of three boys and lives with them and her husband in an antique log cabin on Lookout Mountain. She works with her husband and brother-in-law at Walden Log Homes, where they build homes with antique, hand-hewn logs that are all at least 100 years old. Their Web site is www.waldenloghomes.com.

Gary Earl Ross is a writing professor at the University at Buffalo EOC. His books include *The Wheel of Desire, Shimmerville,* and the children's tale *Dots.* He owns the Web site The Writer's Den (www.angelfire.com/journal/garyearlross).

Trina Schaetz is a writer, editor, and teacher who lives in Wisconsin with her husband and two daughters. She is a graduate of Wheaton College and enjoys swimming, photography, and getting together with her friends and family. She has been published in *Christian Parenting Today, Kid's Ministry* magazine, and *Milwaukee* magazine.

Betty Ann Webster is a retired psychiatric social worker and writer, confirmed Berkeleyite, and addicted traveler who lived in India almost forty years ago and has returned there at least ten times in the intervening years. She has three children, four grandchildren, and two great-grandchildren and would be delighted to hear from you at bettyann@pop.lmi.net.

Marvin J. Wolf is the author of a dozen nonfiction books and hundreds of magazine articles. He has recently altered course to become a screenwriter. Book excerpts, magazine stories, sample scripts can be seen at www.marvwolf.com.

About the Author

BORN AND RAISED IN CANADA, Steve Zikman is the coauthor of *Chicken Soup for the Traveler's Soul* and *Chicken Soup for the Nature Lover's Soul* and author of *The Power of Travel: A Passport to Adventure, Discovery and Growth.*

A certified self-esteem facilitator and keynote speaker, Steve helps audiences shift their perspective, conquer their fears, and embrace life's challenges.

Steve has appeared on hundreds of national and international radio and television programs on various networks including ABC, CBS, NBC, and FOX. A member of the American Society of Journalists and Authors, Steve is a contributor to a variety of online and print media, including *Interline Adventures,* SoulfulLiving.com, and *Personal Journaling.* For further information on Steve Zikman's speaking programs and writings, please visit his Web site at www.GOscape.com.

About UNICEF

THE UNITED NATIONS CHILDREN FUND (UNICEF) consists of more than 7,000 women and men working around the world to promote, protect and advocate for the rights of children through programmes that help children survive and thrive to adulthood, and that provide essential medicines, vaccines educational, health and emergency supplies. In 158 countries and territories, UNICEF brings its influence to bear on the individuals and institutions that serve the youngest generation. For further information, please visit their website at www.UNICEF.org.

About the
Points of Light Foundation

THE POINTS OF LIGHT FOUNDATION, along with the Volunteer Center National Network, is the nation's only nonpartisan and nonprofit organization supporting and organizing the vital work of the millions of volunteers in thousands of communities who are helping to solve our nation's most serious social problems by bringing people and resources together.

The Foundation raises public awareness about the urgent need to solve serious social problems through volunteering; it builds knowledge, skills, and programs for volunteers to succeed; and it provides leadership and local delivery systems to mobilize volunteers in thousands of local communities throughout the country.

For more information, call 1-800-VOLUNTEER or visit www.1-800-VOLUNTEER.org.

Organizations Mentioned in This Book

A Special Wish Foundation   www.spwish.org

Action Without Borders   www.idealist.org

AIDS Walk   www.aidswalk.net

American Heart Association   www.americanheart.org

Automobile Association of America (AAA)   www.aaa.com

Big Brothers Big Sisters of America   www.bbbsa.org

Boys and Girls Club of America   www.bgca.org

Child Development Institute   www.cdipage.com

Climb for the Cure   www.cancerclimb.org

Corporation for National and Community Service
   www.nationalservice.org

Cross-Cultural Solutions   www.crossculturalsolutions.org

Cystic Fibrosis Foundation   www.cff.org

Earthjustice   www.earthjustice.org

Earthwatch Institute   www.earthwatch.org

FamilyEducationNetwork   www.familyeducation.com

For Love of Children   www.floc.org

Grant-A-Wish Foundation   www.grant-a-wish.org

Great Gifts   www.great-gifts.org

Greenpeace   www.greenpeace.org

Habitat for Humanity   www.habitat.org

Healing the Children   www.healingchildren.org

International Volunteer Programs Association
    www.volunteerinternational.org

Kids Can Make A Difference   www.kidscanmakeadifference.org

Make-A-Wish Foundation   www.wish.org

Meals on Wheels   www.mowaa.org

Mothers Against Drunk Driving (MADD)   www.madd.org

National Bone Marrow Donor Program   www.marrow.org

National Bone Marrow Transplant Link   www.nbmtlink.org

National Commission Against Drunk Driving (NCADD)
    www.ncadd.com

National Mentoring Partnership   www.mentoring.org

National Multiple Sclerosis Society   www.nmss.org

National Race for the Cure   www.nationalraceforthecure.org

National Recycling Coalition   www.nrc-recycle.org

Natural Resources Defense Council   www.nrdc.org

National Wildlife Federation   www.nwf.org

Partners Mentoring Association   www.partnersmentoring.org

Peace Corps   www.peacecorps.gov

Points of Light Foundation   www.pointsoflight.org

Prevent Child Abuse America   www.preventchildabuse.org

Red Cross   www.redcross.org

Rotary Club   www.rotary.org

Save Our Environment   www.saveourenvironment.org

Save the Children   www.savethechildren.org

Sierra Club   www.sierraclub.org

Starlight Children's Foundation   www.starlight.org

Students Against Drunk Driving (SADD)   www.saddonline.com

Study Circles Resource Center   www.studycircles.org

Susan G. Komen Breast Cancer Foundation   www.komen.org

Teach for America   www.teachforamerica.org

Teen Politics   www.teenpolitics.com

Teen Power Politics   www.teenpowerpolitics.com

Time to Recycle   www.timetorecycle.org

UNICEF   www.unicef.org

United Way of America   www.unitedway.org

USA WEEKEND Magazine   www.usaweekend.com

Volunteers for Peace   www.vfp.org

What Kids Can Do   www.whatkidscando.org

World Hunger Year   www.worldhungeryear.org

World Wildlife Fund   www.worldwildlife.org

YouthNOISE   www.youthnoise.com

Permissions

Sources

The Doing Good "call to action" material was gathered from a variety of sources. We would like to acknowledge the many individuals and organizations whose helpful work may be found in this book:

Know What to Say in Medical Emergencies (page 43): from *The Worst Is Over: What to Say When Every Moment Counts* by Judith Acosta and Judith Simon Prager (Jodere Group, ©2002).

Learn CPR (page 44): Reprinted with permission of Dr. Mickey Eisenberg and www.learncpr.org, ©2003. Graphics re-created by Robert Fung with permission.

Learn Emergency Driving Techniques (page 51): from the *North Carolina Department of Motor Vehicles Driver Handbook,* chapter 4, ©2004.

Keep an Emergency Safety Kit in Your Car (page 53): Reprinted with permission of Mike Bradshaw, ©2004.

Practice Fire Prevention (page 58): Reprinted with permission of Sheriff Larry Campbell and the Leon County Sheriff's Office, Tallahassee, Florida, ©2001.

Things Kids Have Done to Make a Difference (page 73): Reprinted with permission of Kids Can Make A Difference, ©1999.

Make a Difference in the Lives of the Homeless/What Children Can Do for the Homeless (page 79): Reprinted with permission of Rabbi Charles A. Kroloff, ©2004.

Things Kids Have Done to Help the Homeless (page 87): from www.hud.gov.

Be a Good Volunteer Coach (page 87): Reprinted with permission of Mark Landrum, www.thecoachingcorner.com, ©1998.

Learn More about Becoming a Foster Parent (page 91):
Reprinted with permission of For Love of Children,
www.floc.org, ©2003.

Get Involved in Politics/Write to Your Local Politician (page
96): Reprinted with permission of the Eastern Ontario Child
Poverty Resource Network and the Social Planning Council of
Ottawa, ©2004.

Get Involved in Politics/Learn How to Get Teens More Involved
(page 98): Reprinted with permission of Rosalie J. Bakken and
the University of Nebraska Cooperative Extension, ©2002.

Become a Mentor (page 111): from "Making a Difference: An
Impact Study of Big Brothers Big Sisters of America" (1995),
www.cityimpact.com and www.mentorship-wisemen.org.

Learn More about Self-Esteem and How It Affects Teens (page
117): from www.indiaparenting.com and www.hartshosp.org.

Tips for Increasing a Teen's Self-Esteem (page 117): Reprinted
with permission of Dr. Robert Myers, ©2000.

Help Prevent Child Abuse and Neglect (page 122): Reprinted
with permission of Prevent Child Abuse America, ©2003.

Trick-or-Treat for UNICEF (page 139): Written by Laura L.
Meehan. Reprinted with permission of the Family Education
Network (www.fen.com), ©2000–2004.

Create a Neighborly Needs Day (page 141): Reprinted with
permission of Trina Schaetz, ©2001.

Ways to Prevent Drunk Driving (page 149–152): Reprinted
with permission of the National Commission Against Drunk
Driving (NCADD), ©2004.

Note: We have used our best efforts to acknowledge all references
and contributions in this book. If we have inadvertently omitted a
reference, please let us know and we will correct it in the next
edition.

Index